Praise for *Are You Coachable?*

"Are You Coachable?"(Title): is a compelling exploration of how openness to feedback and guidance can transform one's life. Let's face it, setting aside personal ego and our inherent success bias can be a real challenge for many of us in the business world. The key to understanding how to address that challenge is by learning to cultivate an internal coachable mindset. Embracing that mindset can lead to a significant impact in one's performance and achievement. This book is an invaluable resource for anyone committed to their self-improvement journey, offering profound insights into the power of being coachable."

**John Geshay, certified Executive
Business Coach, FocalPoint,Int'l.**

"Are You Coachable?" is a clear, practical, and extremely relevant book for anyone who wants to be coached/mentored, and for anyone who is a Coach or Mentor. It presents not only the value of being coachable but gives clear ways to evaluate if you currently are or are not coachable. Once you understand where you are, it presents clear and applicable steps for you to become coachable so you can receive the full benefit of being coached. Excellent data, case studies, and great questions are found throughout, making this a 'must have' for those who want to receive all that Coaching can provide."

**Dave Kobelin, ICF PCC, Director of Training,
Awyken Coach Training, Executive Coach,
Excellent Cultures Inc. Owner, ClarityCoach**

"Dr. Coker has an unbelievable way of bringing personal growth and maturity into focus. The combination of the assessment and how to apply it is brilliant! Reflection questions at the end of each chapter allowed me to gain more profound clarity and have meaningful conversations about each stage in my journey. This book is a must-read for you and your entire team!"

**Krystal Parker, President, U.S. &
Central Florida Christian Chambers of Commerce**

"Wow! Chuck's book, "Are You Coachable", is a winner for anyone who longs for the wisdom and personal insights to confirm their ultimate calling and help them grow their lives. Few can maximize the wisdom we all need to be certain of how to apply your talents and abilities, like Chuck. So, fasten your seat belt as Chuck helps you fulfill your life's purpose by preparing you and giving you examples of how to maximize your potential."

**John F. Beehner, Author and Founder of
Wise Counsel, a CEO roundtable**

"Dr. Chuck Coker, in his marvelous book, "Are You Coachable?", provides us fertile soil in which to grow our own understanding of what it means to experience one's full potential in their lives. With the skill of a master teacher and storyteller, he guides us by combining information with case studies that make these principles come to life. I guarantee you'll relate in a very personal way as you live through each discovery. And, because of Dr. Coker's gentle touch, when their story is over, you will find that you will have a new and remarkably comprehensive understanding of your own unfulfilled potential. It will change your life!"

**Dr. S. Bryan Hickox, EMMY Winning
Television & Film Producer**

"Writing is a big part of many individuals' responsibilities. Yet, it takes a special calling and courage to convey in writing a road-map to growth and development for readers. Dr. Coker steps up to the challenge in his new book, "Are You Coachable?" Growth requires time, effort, passion, perseverance, and spending time investing in others. Readers will be filled with gratitude as they discover simple tools to develop their potential"

Mary Anne Jacobs, CEO,
Girl Scouts of Gateway Council, FL

"The models and steps provided in "Are You Coachable"" are useful both retrospectively as well as prospectively. Like any good map, it's comforting to gain the perspective of knowing where one is, has been, and where to go. Without this, we're lost in place and apt to live small, insecure lives. Don't just read this book. Study and apply it as a guidebook rich in wisdom to live into increasing expression of who you in order to maximize your potential."

Kevin W. McCarthy, Co-Creator of ONPURPOSE.
me for finding your 2-word purpose in life

Are You Coachable?

hawkeye.pro

Book Cover: Hawkeye

Interior Design: Albatross Book Co.

First edition 2024

Are You Coachable?

THE SCIENCE OF A GROWTH MINDSET

Chuck Coker, Phd, SPHR

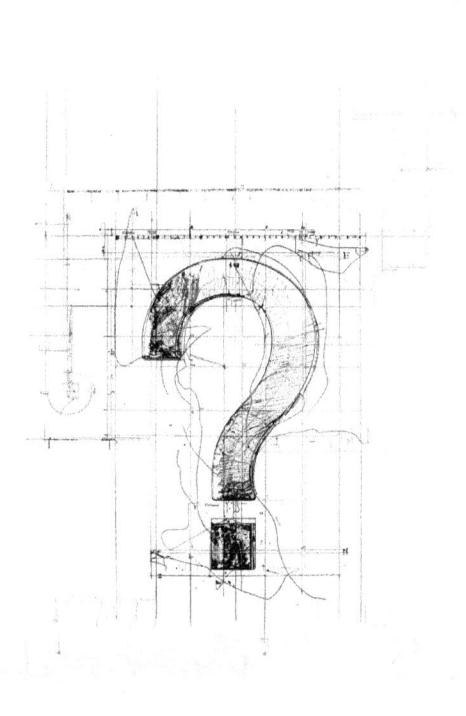

Contents

FOREWORD

Understanding what coaching is and isn't is important when considering coaching as a tool to benefit your life. Knowing the differences and similarities between it and other services that offer personalized help can allow you to make an informed decision, as well as avoid confusion. This is especially true when it comes to coaching and mentoring.

Coaching, as defined by the International Coach Federation (ICF), is a partnership between coach and client in a thought-provoking and creative process that inspires clients to maximize their personal and professional potential. Unlike mentoring, where the mentor often provides advice and direction based on their experience, coaching focuses on empowering clients to find their own solutions. When in the coach position, a coach refrains from telling the client what to do. Instead, the coach helps the client uncover what is truly important to them, understand the reasons behind these values, and determine the actions they need to take.

Over the course of a coaching relationship, typically three to six months, trust and rapport are built between the coach and the client. As this relationship deepens, the client comes to see the coach as a trustworthy partner who is committed to their growth and best interests. In this context of mutual respect and trust, the coach may occasionally step out of the strict coaching role and offer their own perspective or share relevant experiences. This shift into a more mentor-like role is not typical of pure coaching but can be valuable if both parties clearly communicate and agree upon it.

This flexible approach, where a coach may briefly wear a "mentor hat," can be particularly effective in certain situations where the client benefits from the coach's expertise or advice. As long as this role shift is understood and agreed upon, it enhances the coaching experience, allowing the client to receive tailored guidance while still maintaining the self-directed nature of the coaching process. Ultimately, this blend of coaching and mentoring, when done with integrity and clarity, further empowers the client on their journey toward achieving their goals.

—David Kobelin
ICF

Introduction

I hope this book will inspire you. Throughout our lives we often need to check in with ourselves regarding how coachable we are. Or perhaps we become aware suddenly that we need help understanding ourselves and some of the possible ways we have become our own obstacle to growth. This book is written to inspire and guide readers towards personal and professional growth by developing the characteristics of a coachable person. Throughout, I share specific ways to uncover and address potential blind spots in dealing with others, how to embrace feedback, seek out the right coach or mentor, build resilience, hold ourselves accountable, and learn from failure.

I've constructed the book with some scientific truths in mind. Hermann Ebbinghaus (1850 – 1909) was a German psychologist who pioneered the experimental study of memory. He is known for his discovery of the forgetting curve and the spacing effect; he was also the first person to describe the learning curve. Ebbinghaus found that people forget most of what they learn within the first few hours after learning it. After a day or two, they typically forget around 75% of what was learned. And after a week, people may only remember around 20% of what they learned.

Thankfully, there are a few things we can do to improve our ability to remember information. One strategy is to break down large pieces of information into smaller, more manageable chunks. Another is to use mnemonic devices, such as acronyms or rhymes, to help you remember information. You can also improve your memory by practicing recall and by getting enough sleep. The forgetting curve is a good reminder that we need to be pro-active about learning and remembering information.

I've created quick, short chapters, with ideas woven together. I encourage you to spend time with the ideas and try to see yourself in the case studies. Take time to absorb and ponder the concepts in each chapter.

Here are other key principles to apply from Ebbinghaus' theory:

- Take time. Give yourself space to ponder.
- Find connection to your own story through the examples in this book.
- Review the ideas again after a few days and see what new understanding rises in your mind.
- Get good rest!

Ebbinghaus's experiments determined that physiological factors, such as stress and sleep, can play a significant part in how well information is retained. People often experience this as a vicious cycle. When they feel stress, it makes it harder to remember, which creates even more stress. There's also strong evidence to suggest that sleep can help the brain to sort and store information.

Overall, the strategy for "Are You Coachable?" is to inspire and guide you toward becoming the best version of yourself so you can achieve greater success and fulfillment in life. You must ask yourself: "How important is it for me to be teachable and/or coachable?" And then, "Am I willing to invest in myself?" In the chapters ahead, you will learn valuable skills and tools to develop the characteristics of a coachable person. By committing yourself to becoming more coachable, you can find more success in achieving your personal and professional goals.

CHAPTER 1

The Importance of Being Coachable

In today's fast-paced world, the ability to learn and adapt quickly is becoming increasingly important. Whether in your personal or professional life, you are constantly faced with new challenges and opportunities for growth. Being coachable—that is, being willing to seek feedback, guidance, and new ideas—is a key factor in achieving success and fulfillment.

But why is being coachable so important? For starters, it allows you to learn from the experiences of others and avoid common pitfalls. It also helps you identify your strengths and weaknesses and create a plan for improvement. In short, being coachable enables you to take control of your own growth and development.

As social beings, humans have always depended on each other for survival, well-being, and personal growth. We rely on others for a wide range of things, including emotional support, companionship, knowledge, skills, resources, and more. Here are a few thoughts on why depending on others is necessary:

Four hundred years ago, John Donne penned this quote in his "John Donne's Devotions" (1624):

> *"No man is an island, entire of itself; every man is a piece of the continent, a part of the main."*

You see, no one can survive in isolation. Humans are interconnected and interdependent beings. So, your well-being is closely tied to the well-being of those around you. Everyone has their own unique set of skills, talents, and interests. By depending on others, you can take advantage of their strengths and expertise while also contributing to the collective effort.

There is power when people work together. You can accomplish more when you work with others than you could by working alone. By pooling resources, you can achieve goals that would otherwise be difficult or impossible to accomplish. In the workplace, for example, when team members divide the labor or assign individuals to specialized tasks, the team can achieve greater efficiency and productivity based on each individual's unique skill set. Based on studies by Bruce W. Tuckman in 1965, teams will go through the growth stages of "Forming, Storming, Norming and Performing" more quickly and efficiently.

While it's important to be self-sufficient to some degree, depending on others is a natural and necessary part of human life. The key is to find a balance between independence and interdependence, and to build healthy and mutually beneficial relationships with those around you.

Another benefit of being coachable is that it allows you to build strong relationships with others. When you are open to feedback and guidance, you demonstrate a willingness to listen and learn from others. This can lead to more meaningful connections with friends, family, coworkers, and mentors.

The fact is that you can learn a lot from others, whether it's through mentorship, collaboration, or simply observing their behavior. Depending on others can help you grow and develop as an individual. Humans are social creatures who thrive on emotional connections with others. It's only natural to depend on others for emotional support, validation, and a sense of belonging—especially when facing challenging circumstances in life.

At the same time, being coachable does not mean blindly accepting everything others tell you. Rather, it means being receptive to new ideas and perspectives, while also using your own judgment and critical thinking skills. It's about striking a balance between being open-minded and discerning.

Being open-minded means being receptive to new ideas and experiences without automatically rejecting them. It involves a willingness to consider different perspectives and opinions, even if they challenge your existing beliefs.

Being discerning, on the other hand, means being able to evaluate and judge the quality and value of the information or ideas you encounter. It involves critical thinking and the ability to differentiate between fact and fiction, truth and lies, valid arguments and fallacious ones.

You need to be both open-minded and discerning because these qualities complement each other. If you are too open-minded without being discerning, you may fall for false or misleading information and make poor decisions as a result. On the other hand, if you are overly discerning without being open-minded, you may become closed off to new and potentially valuable perspectives and miss out on opportunities for growth and learning.

By being both open-minded and discerning, you can approach new ideas and information with a critical yet open eye, evaluating them based on their merits and considering their potential value. If there is any question or doubt on your part, don't hesitate to take the time to reason through the challenge or directions—you will usually be glad you did. This can help you make more informed decisions, broaden your perspective, and ultimately boost your personal growth and development.

Being coachable is an essential skill for anyone looking to achieve their goals and live a fulfilling life because no one has all the answers. Try to have an open mindset and be willing to improve because every person has weaknesses that will require changes to improve their personal performance as well as their chosen profession. And change is inevitable. If you are coachable, you will be able to adapt to new situations and challenges because you'll recognize there is always room to grow and become a better individual.

In the chapters ahead, you'll learn more about what it means to be coachable, and you will also receive practical tips for developing this important skill. Each topic we address will better position you for achieving your goals and becoming the individual you imagined yourself to be. While some concepts or suggestions may seem repetitive at times, the key principles are interrelated and interdependent. Together, they build synergy and enhance the process of helping you become more coachable.

Defining Vision

For starters, having a clear vision of who you are and how you are gifted will provide greater clarity surrounding your assets. With that knowledge, you will have a better sense of direction and purpose in life. This vision will help you set goals and make decisions that align with your values, beliefs, and aspirations. Having a strong sense of direction can bring greater meaning and fulfillment to your life.

One of the best things about clarifying your vision is that it can boost your self-esteem and confidence. When you see yourself making progress towards your goals, you develop a sense of pride in your accomplishments and an increased belief in your ability to achieve even more.

Having a clear vision will also improve your relationships with others. When you have a clear sense of who you are and what you stand for, you attract people who share your values and beliefs. This can lead to more authentic and fulfilling relationships.

Most importantly, gaining a clearer vision will help you leave a positive impact on the world. When you are true to yourself and pursue your passions, you can inspire others to do the same. You can make a difference in the lives of those around you and leave a legacy that reflects the person you were created to be.

As you dive further into the material, you will also examine some of the common roadblocks to being coachable—such as fear of feedback and resistance to change. By addressing these challenges head-on, you can begin to overcome them and unlock your full potential. While it may appear that some people "look" better than you, have more potential than you, or possess skills you wish you had, this is NOT always true. As you become the person you were designed to be, your individuality will stand out in the crowd, and you will earn the respect of those who are discerning and insightful.

It's important to note that being coachable is not something that comes naturally to everyone. It's a skill that requires practice and effort, and it may not always be easy. However, the rewards of being coachable are well worth the effort. By embracing a coachable mindset, you can open yourself up to new opportunities, experiences, and insights.

As you move through each stage of this book, you'll explore some of the key characteristics of coachable people, such as humility, motivation, and a desire to learn and grow. You'll also learn more about the role of feedback, mentorship, and support networks in developing a coachable mindset.

Key Insights

Whether you're a seasoned professional, a student just starting out, or someone looking to make a change, the lessons in this book can help you unlock your full potential and reach your goals. So, let's get started!

Reflection Questions:

1. How can being coachable benefit you personally and professionally?

2. Have you ever resisted feedback or coaching? Why?

3. What are some common misconceptions about being coachable?

4. What are some examples of successful people who are coachable?

5. How do you hope your life will be different if you decide to complete a coaching program?

How do you practice being coachable?

1. *Listen actively and be open to feedback:* Being coachable requires a willingness to listen to constructive criticism, even if it is not what you want to hear. When receiving feedback, try to be fully present and engaged, actively listening to what the other person is saying without interrupting or becoming defensive. Then, take the feedback to heart and use it to improve your skills and performance.

2. *Embrace a growth mindset:* Adopting a growth mindset is essential to being coachable. This means being open to new ideas, recognizing that there is always room for improvement, and viewing mistakes and setbacks as opportunities to learn and grow. Embracing a growth mindset will help

you approach coaching with a positive attitude, knowing that every interaction has the potential to make you a better person.

3. ***Take action and follow through:*** Being coachable requires more than just listening and receiving feedback. It also means taking action in response to the feedback you receive and following through on commitments to improve. This requires discipline and accountability, as well as a willingness to put in the hard work necessary to achieve your goals. Remember, a coach can guide you, but it is ultimately up to you to take ownership of your development and make the necessary changes.

CHAPTER 2

The Characteristics of a Coachable Person

Are you ready to find out if you're coachable? We invite you to take the "The Coachability Index" assessment at https://www.lifethrive.com/coachability-assessment/.

Scan here!

Use this coupon code: d48a52b653 to take the assessment for free. Upon completion, you will understand your results more thoroughly and it serves as a guide as you navigate through this guide. It's our gift to you for purchasing the book, and we hope it accelerates your growth and development. If you need further help or assistance, please contact us at info@lifethrive.com.

What does it mean to be coachable? At its core, being coachable means seeking feedback as well as being receptive to feedback, guidance, or new ideas. But what are the specific characteristics that make someone coachable? In this chapter, you'll learn some of the key traits of coachable people from all aspects of their personality. You will have the opportunity to consider all three dimensions of coachability and how they can impact you as an individual.

If you refer to the Coachability Summary Page of your **The Coachability Index**, you will see your scores in the three overarching areas of coachability, as well as in each of their sub-categories as defined below:

INTRAPERSONAL

-Expressed Humility

-Motivation

INTERPERSONAL

-Seeking Feedback

-Feedback Receptivity

IMPLEMENTATION

-Response Motive

-Response to Feedback

Let's take a few moments to unpack some of these characteristics of a coachable person.

INTRAPERSONAL: Expressed Humility

One of the most important characteristics of coachable people is expressed humility. Humility is an internal quality that allows you to recognize your own limitations and weaknesses, and to be open to feedback and guidance from others. Expressed humility, on the other hand, is an external or outward demonstration or display of humility, with statements, behaviors, or gestures that communicate humility to others. When you approach situations with a respectful attitude, you're more likely to learn from your mistakes and grow as an individual.

In March of 2020, Jake Alexander Weiss submitted his doctoral dissertation on "Employee Coachability and Managerial Coaching in Organizations" to the faculty at DePaul University.[1] (Some of his findings were used to create several questions and measurements for the Coachability index). On page 106 we find a key point. The leading correlation in his findings clearly stated that: "*. . . expressed humility positively relates to an employee's coachability. Research indicates that humble individuals seek more feedback in order to see themselves more accurately through interactions with others. A component of expressed humility—teachability—manifests in individuals who display an openness to learning, feedback and new ideas from others.*"

INTRAPERSONAL: Motivation

Coachable people are motivated to improve themselves and achieve their goals. Without motivation, you may be willing to receive feedback but may not have the drive to take the necessary steps to improve. When you are internally driven to act on feedback, you are more likely to put in the time and effort necessary to make changes.

Additionally, motivation can help you stay committed to the process of improving. Receiving feedback can sometimes be difficult or even uncomfortable, but if you are determined to improve, you are more likely to push through any challenges or setbacks that may arise. Motivation is essential for a coachable

---

1   Weiss, Jake Alexander, "An Examination of Employee Coachability and Managerial Coaching in Organizations" (2020). *College of Science and Health Theses and Dissertations*. 323. https://via.library.depaul.edu/csh_etd/323

person because it drives action, helps maintain commitment, and supports the ongoing process of improvement.

A motivated person has a clear sense of direction and purpose, and they're willing to put in the hard work and effort required to succeed. Motivation can help you stay focused and committed, even in the face of challenges or setbacks.

INTERPERSONAL: Seeking Feedback

Coachable people have a strong desire to learn and grow. Are you curious about the world around you and eager to expand your knowledge and skills? A thirst for knowledge and growth can help you stay open-minded and receptive to new ideas and perspectives.

When you seek feedback, it shows that you know you need help identifying your blind spots. Feedback provides an opportunity to see yourself, your work, and your relationships from a different perspective, revealing things that may have been otherwise missed and allowing you to refine your work and make necessary changes.

Seeking feedback can also increase self-awareness and help you better understand your strengths and weaknesses. Only then can you be comfortable when leaders hold you accountable for your work and your goals. When you know you will be receiving feedback, it increases your motivation and sense of responsibility for achieving your objectives.

INTERPERSONAL: Feedback Receptivity

It's important to remember that everyone is unique and has their own reasons for seeking feedback and will respond to it in different ways. With this in mind, when you are in the position of providing feedback to others, try to be respectful of other people's perspectives and understand that they may not always follow the advice provided—even if it seems like the best course of action to you. Likewise, be aware that in some cases you may seek feedback from others but not apply the wisdom or direction passed on to you. These are examples of what Weiss described on page 109 of his dissertation when he pointed out: *"However, the instrumental motive [seeking feedback] does not relate to feedback receptivity."*

Sometimes, people seek feedback not because they are looking for direction or guidance, but because they want validation for their ideas or decisions. When you find yourself in this frame of mind, you may not be receptive to following a different direction because you are already committed to your present course of action. This can be especially true if you do not respect or trust the person giving the feedback—even though they have a greater level of expertise. You may feel that the feedback is not relevant to your situation, or that the person giving the feedback does not have the necessary expertise or experience to provide useful guidance.

At times, you may seek feedback as a way of gathering information—but you may not be ready to follow through on the advice provided, or you might have different priorities or goals than the person providing the feedback. As a result, you may not be receptive to following the direction provided because it does not align with your own objectives or values. But in order to become a truly coachable person, you can practice being receptive to any feedback that is helpful, regardless of the source. And that may be the difference between success and failure.

APPLICATION: Response Motive

Developing a strong response motive will make you open to—and eager to apply—guidance that makes your life better, or that helps you obtain new objectives. You simply must be willing to try new concepts rather than fearing the unknown. Flexing your response motive muscles can help you focus on what is truly important and seek out feedback that helps you take action steps toward your goals.

If your response motive is low, it may be due to a lack of clarity about what you are trying to achieve. You may struggle in this area if you lack self-confidence, fear failure, feel you have a lack of support, or have high-stress factors in your life. But those challenges can be met when you identify the steps to building motivation—and your coach must be "all in" if they are going to help you find that.

When you are being coached, in most cases you will realize the need to break down your goals into smaller, more manageable steps that can build momentum—otherwise known as SMART goals. (We will define and illustrate this in chapters ahead.) This will allow you to visualize the emotions associated with that success, further increasing your motivation. This can inspire you to seek role models or individuals who have achieved similar goals. Learning from their experience will only heighten your level of inspiration and motivation.

APPLICATION: Response to Feedback

Coachable people have a growth mindset. They believe that their most basic abilities can be developed through dedication and hard work because brains and talent are just a starting point. They are willing to accept feedback as a learning opportunity. It is essential to understand the benefit of implementing feedback, regardless of whether it is for personal growth, professional development, or achieving your goals. Breaking the objective into smaller, actionable steps makes it more manageable; that's why most coachable people look to SMART goals for the motivation they need to move quickly.

Highly coachable people act on the feedback as soon as possible. Procrastination can lead to a loss of both opportunity and motivation, which makes it more difficult for you to act on feedback later. As an antidote to procrastination, be sure to celebrate progress. Acknowledge and celebrate your wins, no matter how small, while learning from your mistakes. Recognizing your achievements can help increase your motivation and give you a sense of accomplishment.

Why Self-Awareness Matters

In addition to these six key characteristics that we have discussed so far, it is vital to understand the value of self-awareness and reflection when it comes to coachability. When you have a clear understanding of your own strengths and weaknesses, you'll be more open to feedback that can help you improve. Self-awareness helps you take ownership of your own growth and development. That is why we measure the six dimensions of coachability in the Coachability Index.

Self-awareness also motivates you to be a good listener. When you're attentive and receptive to the perspectives and feedback of others, you can more effectively communicate your own thoughts and ideas. This skill helps you build strong relationships with others and learn from the experiences of those around you. Stay tuned for more on this topic in the next chapter.

Key Insights

Coachable people possess a unique set of characteristics that enable them to learn and grow in a meaningful way. Don't be overly concerned about your present scores, just understand this is where you are beginning—not finishing. Coaching will help you develop those areas that need improvement. By embracing your present traits and developing a coachable mindset, you can unlock your full potential and achieve greater success and fulfillment in life. In the following chapters, you can explore how to develop these characteristics and become more coachable.

I want to share one closing thought before ending this chapter. For over 30+ years I have assessed and coached people in the area of growth and development, administering over 100,000 different assessments. In only four cases have I identified individuals who simply did not have what was necessary to attain reasonable objectives. Where you are or what your scores are important for one reason and one reason only—to identify your strengths and weaknesses so you can bring clarity to a plan to achieve your goals. Don't let anyone tell you anything differently.

Case Study: Tom

Tom suffered from social anxiety disorder as well as what appeared to be a learning disability when he was referred to me by a prominent psychologist. After graduating from a prestigious university, he sunk into depression because he could not find a job and soon moved back home with his parents for several years. After assessing Tom, I shared his results with him, illustrating that he was both capable and intelligent enough to do almost anything he wanted to do. He just needed to realize his gifting was different from what he thought he wanted to do.

Within six months Tom was registered for his master's degree in an unrelated field. After completing his first semester he quickly identified new subject matter that allowed him to work within his strengths. Tom graduated Magna Cum Laude and has multiple job opportunities now open to him.

Reflection Questions:

1. What characteristics do you already possess that make you coachable?

2. In what ways can curiosity and a desire to learn help you be more coachable?

3. What is the difference between being coachable and being a people-pleaser?

4. What are some common traits of people who are resistant to coaching?

5. How can being coachable improve your relationships with others?

How can you practice the six aspects of being coachable?

1. **Cultivate humility:** One of the key elements of being coachable is having a humble attitude. This means being open to the fact that you may not know everything and recognizing that there is always room for improvement. To cultivate humility, practice listening to others without interrupting or dismissing their ideas. Seek out opportunities to learn from those who have more experience or expertise than you do.

2. **Stay motivated:** To be coachable, it's important to stay motivated and committed to your goals. This means setting clear objectives for yourself, and staying focused on the steps you need to take to achieve them. When working with a coach, be open and honest about your aspirations and any obstacles you may be facing. Stay engaged in the coaching process even when it gets challenging.

3. **Seek and receive feedback:** Another important element of being coachable is seeking and receiving feedback from others. This means actively seeking out constructive criticism, even if it may be uncomfortable or difficult to hear. When receiving feedback, stay receptive and avoid becoming defensive or dismissive. Instead, try to listen with an open

mind, ask clarifying questions, and work to understand how you can use the feedback to improve your performance.

4. **Maintain a positive attitude:** To be coachable, it's important to maintain a positive attitude and approach coaching with a growth mindset. This means embracing challenges as opportunities for learning, staying optimistic in the face of setbacks, and remaining open to new ideas and perspectives. When receiving feedback, try to focus on the opportunities for growth and improvement, rather than becoming discouraged or defensive.

5. **Respond appropriately to feedback:** Finally, coachable people respond appropriately to feedback. This means taking the feedback seriously and using it to make concrete changes in your behavior or performance. If you've already worked with a coach, you've probably received feedback. It also means communicating effectively with your coach, seeking clarification when needed, and following through on any commitments you make to improve. Remember, the coaching relationship is a two-way street, and your coach is there to support and guide you. But you are ultimately responsible for your own development.

CHAPTER 3

Cultivating Self-Awareness

The first step to emotional intelligence and growth

Self-awareness involves having a clear understanding of one's own behaviors, mindsets, priorities, and motivations—*from other people's perspectives*! However, it can be difficult to gain this understanding without the help of assessment tools. In this chapter, you will learn why coaches use assessments that accelerate growth and add deeper value to their clients. Additionally, it's important to recognize the critical role of self-awareness when it comes to increasing your emotional intelligence—and that is what most leaders look for and value in employees, even more than technical expertise.

Self-awareness is considered the foundation for building emotional intelligence. Without it, you will not have the ability to recognize and understand your own emotions, thoughts, and behaviors—or why others react to you the way they do. Without this ability, you may struggle to identify your emotional reactions and may have trouble regulating or managing them effectively due to the rationalization of your own actions. That is why a logical, empirical, and objective approach is far superior to "what someone thinks about themselves."

Self-awareness is also crucial in developing emotional intelligence because it allows you to recognize how your emotions and behaviors affect others. This understanding can help you manage your emotional responses, leading to more positive interactions with others. Additionally, self-awareness helps you recognize your strengths and weaknesses, which enhances your personal and professional development.

The Role of Assessments in Coaching

Assessments and coaching are two different but complementary processes that can provide valuable insights and help you reach your goals. Let's take a closer look at how they work together.

Assessments provide objective information about your strengths, weaknesses, personality traits, skills, and behaviors. **Coaching,** on the other hand, is a process that helps you identify and achieve your goals, overcome obstacles, and develop new skills and behaviors. A coach can help you create action plans, provide guidance and feedback, and hold you accountable for making progress towards your goals.

Assessments save valuable time during the coaching process by helping your coach identify areas where you need to focus. Assessments also serve as a communication tool between you and your coach. A coach who understands and can apply the results of an assessment can explain areas that need improvement, what to focus on, and what outcomes to expect. This saves time and ensures that both you and your coach are on the same page.

The information gathered from assessments can help your coach tailor their coaching approach to your specific needs and preferences. Additionally, assessment results can provide a clear picture of your starting point, so your coach can track your development over time and determine if their coaching approach is effective or if it needs to be modified.

Therefore, assessment results provide valuable information to inform and guide the coaching process. By combining the insights gained from an assessment with the guidance and support provided by a coach, you can make more informed decisions, gain new perspectives, and develop the skills and behaviors necessary to achieve your goals. A coach who does not use assessments will likely struggle to help you define your goals and the necessary steps to reach them.

The type of assessment tools that are considered most helpful are those that measure behavioral traits, values, motivations, coachability, and emotional intelligence. Each of these dimensions will help you improve your interpersonal relationships, decision-making, and self-awareness. When used in conjunction with self-reflection and feedback from others, you will gain a more complete understanding of yourself and your potential for growth. In the paragraphs ahead, you can learn about several types of assessments and the value they can bring to both you and your coach.

Simple, minimally complex behavioral assessments are preferable for most people who seek out coaching—after all, this is not an exercise in making you a psychologist. However, your coach, if you have decided to engage one, must determine your level of coachability in order to manage expectations during the coaching process. By now, you should have completed your **Coachability Index** at: (https://www.lifethrive.com/coachability-assessment/). Share that if you decide to engage a professional coach. If you are strong in some categories and weak in others, the coach will know exactly how to tailor their coaching strategy.

Scan here!

Other Common Coaching Assessments Your Coach May Want To Use

Behavioral assessments help you better understand your interactional strengths, weaknesses, and tendencies as well as how those traits affect your interactions with others. These assessments often define potential areas of conflict with others and may reveal how you will approach a specific role or job. One of the most common and easy to understand behavioral tools is **DISC**. It provides a simple, easy-to-interpret understanding of your personality traits and how others perceive you.

Values assessments, like the **Motivators** profile, can help individuals understand their core values and priorities, which are most often culturally generated. Understanding one's values is important because they influence one's behavior and decision-making. Through this tool, an individual can gain insight into what is most important to them and how their values may conflict with others. This can lead to a better understanding of oneself and increased self-awareness.

Motivational assessments, such as the **Habit Story**, can help you understand your core values and priorities. By examining your motivations, you can identify what drives you and gives you a sense of purpose. This can help you make more informed decisions about your career and personal life or identify areas for personal growth and development.

Emotional intelligence assessments, such as the *The EI Index,* can help you understand your emotional strengths and weaknesses. Emotional intelligence involves the ability to recognize, understand, and manage your own emotions, as well as the emotions of others. Taking an emotional intelligence assessment can give you a better understanding of your present emotional intelligence level so you can identify the steps necessary for improvement.

While this may seem like overkill, using multiple assessments can provide a comprehensive and reliable view of your strengths, weaknesses, and development areas. The insights gained from multiple assessments can also enhance the feedback process and improve your motivation throughout the coaching process. If you are ready to invest in yourself, getting a comprehensive view of yourself through multiple assessments can help you get a reasonable return on your coaching investment.

The Value of Being Understood

Hopefully by now you have seen the value that a professional coach can bring to your life. If you have not already engaged one, I strongly encourage you to consider it, as they can significantly accelerate your growth and development.

There are a number of reasons why you want to ensure a coach understands your coachability, behaviors, values, motivations, and emotional intelligence—otherwise, the coaching process will likely take longer, produce marginal results, and end up being less fulfilling. Here are a few of those reasons:

Understanding your behaviors and values...

- Helps the coach build rapport and establish a connection with you, which is essential for effective coaching.
- Helps the coach identify any obstacles or challenges that may hinder your progress.
- Gives the coach insights to help you stay accountable for progress toward your goals.

Understanding your motivations...

- Allows the coach to help you enhance your performance and achieve your goals.
- Allows the coach to encourage your development in areas that are important to you.

Understanding your emotional intelligence...

- Helps the coach establish trust with you, which is critical for a successful coaching relationship.
- Enables the coach to provide effective feedback that is tailored to your needs and preferences.

Case Study: Rashi

Rashi moved to the United States after graduating from college. He managed a manufacturing plant that had been in his family for years. He was used to being a boss and barking out orders to the line workers. His strongly objective nature and cultural background required that he be forceful and direct. This kept the operation moving smoothly and efficiently. Then he moved to the U.S. after marrying an American woman.

His new role required that he interact directly with potential clients who needed help in streamlining their products. His very direct and opinionated approach soon endangered his position and caused his CEO to contact me. Our first meeting was challenging, to say the least! Rashi pushed back on taking assessments. When he learned it was part of the process, he relented. But Rashi struggled with the results.

During our debriefing, I asked him why he moved to the U.S. rather than having his wife move to his homeland. He replied that the U.S. is the land of opportunity and that with hard work and effort he could succeed at higher levels than living off the family business. I agreed with him and emphasized his comment about hard work and effort—especially when it came to self-awareness and its impact on cultivating new clients. Culturally, doing business in the U.S. requires meeting customer expectations, rather than telling them what to do.

Our next meeting was a significant turnaround. He joked about relaying our conversation to his wife and boss, and how they both rebuffed him. With encouragement from the personal and professional sides of his life, and with the realization that relationships and jobs were on the line, Rashi became more receptive to coaching. Soon a plan was in place with specific areas of focus, and progress began.

A year later, Rashi was promoted to president of the new division of his company. His new self-awareness allowed him to regulate his interactions and use his experiential expertise to win new customers at a rate that means the division could easily become the largest in the organization's conglomerate.

Reflection Questions:

1. What do you hope to gain from taking assessments in your coaching process?

2. How do your assessment results align with your personal values and beliefs?

3. In what ways do your assessment results reflect your strengths and weaknesses?

4. What assumptions or biases may be present in your assessment results, and how can you account for them?

5. In what ways do your assessment results challenge or confirm your self-perception?

How can you use your assessments to become more coachable?

1. **Review your assessments:** Take the time to carefully read through your assessments and try to understand the feedback you received. This may involve asking questions or seeking clarification from your coach or evaluator.

2. **Identify areas for improvement:** Once you have a good understanding of your assessments, identify specific areas where you could improve. Look for patterns or recurring themes in the feedback and prioritize the areas where you think you could make the most progress.

3. **Set goals:** Based on your assessment results, set specific and measurable goals that you can work toward. These goals should be focused on the areas where you need to improve and should be realistic and achievable.

4. **Develop an action plan:** Once you have a coach to guide you, they can help you set your goal and develop a plan for how you will achieve them. In addition to working with a coach or mentor, taking courses or training, or practicing specific skills or behaviors will provide deeper insight into your desired goals and objectives..

5. **Monitor your progress:** Regularly check in on your progress toward your goals and make adjustments as needed. Celebrate your successes along the way and use any setbacks as opportunities to learn and grow.

CHAPTER 4

The Role of Expressed Humility

Expressed humility is a key characteristic of coachable people. It's the ability to recognize your own limitations and weaknesses, express them to your coach, and be open to feedback and guidance from others. Unfortunately, it is entirely human to rationalize your behavior and justify your actions which indicates a fixed rather than a growth mindset. While this is normal, it is probably not the pathway to growth and development. Based on the DePaul University study previously quoted in Chapter 2, expressed humility has a relative weight of 69.92% prediction of coachability and that is why it is key to measure this area in a coachability assessment. (Weiss, 2020).[2]

Expressed humility is important for personal and professional growth because it enables you to approach situations with an open mind and be receptive to feedback and constructive criticism. If you maintain this type of unprivileged mindset, you will

---

2   Weiss, Jake Alexander, "An Examination of Employee Coachability and Managerial Coaching in Organizations" (2020). *College of Science and Health Theses and Dissertations. Publication No. 323* (94). https://via.library.depaul.edu/csh_etd/323

continuously learn and improve yourself. By being humble, and expressing your need for input, you are better equipped to grow from your faults or missteps, adapt to changing circumstances, and reach your full potential.

When you express your humility, it means you are willing to acknowledge your limitations and mistakes, which allows you to learn from them and make necessary changes to your behavior or mindset. Humility contributes to a growth mindset instead of a fixed mindset. It also allows you to be more empathetic and understanding of others, which can lead to stronger relationships and collaborations.

In a professional setting, humility can lead to greater success by encouraging you to seek out mentors, collaborate with colleagues, and be open to new ideas and perspectives. Humility can also help you to be a more effective leader by promoting a culture of inclusivity, empowering team members, and fostering an environment of continuous learning and improvement.

But why is humility so important for personal and professional growth?

Learning From Mistakes

Expressed Humility is the ingredient that allows us to learn from our mistakes. Making mistakes is an essential part of the learning process because it allows you to gain new insights and knowledge through trial and error. When you make a mistake, you can identify what went wrong, what didn't work, and what you need to improve upon. By recognizing your errors, you can adjust your approach and try again, incorporating what was learned through your mistakes.

Mistakes also help you develop critical thinking skills and creativity, since you have to think of new solutions to overcome the problems you encounter. Making mistakes forces you to think outside the box, which can lead to new discoveries and innovative ideas.

Moreover, making mistakes allows you to build resilience and learn from failure. You learn that failure is not something to be feared or avoided, but rather an opportunity for growth and improvement. This mindset helps you persevere through challenges and setbacks, ultimately leading to greater success in the long run.

Armed with a willingness to admit that you don't have all the answers, you're more likely to seek out feedback and guidance from others. This feedback can help you identify areas for improvement and develop strategies to overcome weaknesses.

Building Relationships

Expressed humility helps you build strong relationships with others. It promotes open communication and helps you become receptive to the opinions and ideas of others. When you are humble, you are more likely to listen actively and without judgment. This kind of open communication builds trust and strengthens relationships.

Humility also enables you to recognize that you are not the center of the universe and that everyone has their own struggles and challenges. This recognition increases your empathy toward others, so you can better understand their feelings and perspectives and then respond with kindness and compassion. This will allow you to admit when you are wrong and apologize when you make mistakes. This helps to reduce conflicts in relationships and promotes a culture of forgiveness and understanding.

Relationally, when you express humility it enables others to recognize that you don't have all the answers and that you can benefit from their contributions and perspectives.

Another critically important component of humility is that it strengthens respect. Expressed humility involves acknowledging the value and worth of others. Approaching others with humility and appreciation helps to build a strong foundation of mutual respect and understanding. This can lead to more meaningful connections and collaborations, both personally and professionally, as you learn from the perspectives of others and enhance your relationships.

Staying Grounded

Humility allows you to stay grounded and focused on your goals by recognizing your limitations and weaknesses: Humility helps you acknowledge that you are not perfect and there is always room for improvement. This prevents you from becoming overconfident and complacent, which can lead to setbacks and failures.

When you approach others with humility, you are more open to learning from them. You'll recognize that others may have knowledge and skills that you do not possess and be more willing to listen and learn from them. This can help you improve your own abilities and achieve your goals more effectively.

Humility also helps you maintain perspective by recognizing that your goals are just one part of the larger picture. As you grow in humility, you will understand that your success or failure does not define your worth as a person. Maintaining this perspective can help you avoid becoming too focused on your own goals to the exclusion of everything else.

Humility also helps you handle the setbacks that are common in life, which can be critical in managing stress. When you experience setbacks or failures, humility helps you maintain your focus and motivation. Instead of becoming discouraged or blaming others, you can lean into your humility to take responsibility for your mistakes, learn from them, and move forward.

Being willing to admit that you don't know everything can be liberating, and certainly makes it easier to stay open-minded and receptive to new ideas and perspectives. This can help you adapt to changing circumstances and overcome obstacles that may arise along the way.

But developing and expressing your humility is not always easy. However, developing humility is an essential part of becoming more coachable and achieving personal and professional growth.

Self-Reflection

So how can you develop and express your humility properly? Well, it's a lifelong process of self-reflection. Consider your mistakes, weaknesses, and areas that need improvement. Others are not perfect, and neither are you! However, you can learn through active listening—by being open to people who have different experiences and perspectives and seeking to understand their point of view.

Practice gratitude by cultivating a sense of appreciation for the people and things in your life. Recognize that you did not achieve everything on your own, and that you have been helped along the way by others. Then you can embrace your failures, instead of being defensive or making excuses when you make a mistake. Often, people learn more from their mistakes than by doing things right the first time. So take responsibility for your actions and use them as an opportunity to learn and grow.

To maintain a growth mindset, you must stay curious. Try approaching new situations with an open mind and a willingness to learn. Embrace the unknown and be willing to ask questions.

Humility requires that you make an effort to serve others in your community by volunteering or engaging in acts of kindness. Those acts can help you gain perspective and recognize the needs of others.

Key Insights

Both humility and your ability to express it to others is a crucial component of personal and professional growth. So, actively listen to what others have to say, without interrupting or dismissing their perspectives. Seek out feedback and guidance from others and be open to constructive criticism. Finally, express gratitude and appreciation for the people and experiences that have helped you along the way.

By embracing a humble attitude and being open to feedback and guidance from others, you can become more coachable and achieve greater success and fulfillment in your life.

Case Study: Serving Others

Years ago, I was fortunate to have a memorable conversation during a speaking engagement in Washington, D.C. I had the opportunity to share the stage with the late Zig Ziglar. Since Ziglar was a popular motivational speaker who had authored more than 30 books, I asked him why he felt he had achieved success. He looked at me and smiled when answering: "By helping others achieve their objectives." My admiration for Ziglar soared even higher in that moment— this inspiring man could have answered that question in many self-serving ways, but instead his response revealed a habit of putting others first. His response was so different from the world of self-promotion that we live in, that it literally made me stop and rethink my whole approach to business.

Reflection Question:

1. How can humility help you be more open to feedback?

2. What are some benefits of being humble?

3. How can humility help you be more self-aware?

4. What are some clues or warning signs that your ego is getting in the way of your growth?

5. What role does vulnerability play in being humble?

How can you practice applying humility in the growth and development process?

1. **Practice active listening:** Humility begins with being open to different perspectives and ideas. Active listening involves fully engaging with another person's thoughts and feelings without interrupting or judging them. Make a conscious effort to listen to others before speaking and try to understand their point of view.

2. **Acknowledge your limitations:** Recognize that you are not perfect and that there is always room for growth and improvement. Accept feedback gracefully and use it to help you learn and grow. Embrace mistakes as opportunities for growth and avoid blaming others or making excuses for your own shortcomings.

3. **Serve others:** One of the best ways to practice humility is to focus on serving others. Volunteer your time and talents to help those in need and seek opportunities to contribute to your community. By putting others first, you can develop a deeper sense of empathy and compassion.

4. **Cultivate a beginner's mindset:** Approach new situations and experiences with an open mind and a willingness to learn. Avoid preconceived notions or assumptions—instead, ask questions and seek guidance from others. By adopting a beginner's mindset, you can embrace the learning process and develop a deeper understanding of yourself and the world around you.

CHAPTER 5

Overcoming the Fear of Feedback

Receiving feedback is an essential part of being coachable. It's how you learn about your strengths and weaknesses, and how you identify areas for improvement. Without a desire to have input from others, how will you learn? The ability to seek feedback is critical to your growth and development, and that is why it is important to measure it as a key factor of your coachability.

However, many people struggle with the fear of feedback. They worry about criticism, rejection, or failure, and may avoid seeking out feedback altogether. In this chapter, we'll explore some common fears people have about feedback and how to overcome them.

Fear of Criticism

One of the most common fears people have about feedback is the fear of criticism, worrying it will be negative or harsh and damage their self-esteem. To overcome this fear, realize that feedback is not a personal attack but information to help you improve. Focus on the constructive aspects and find ways to incorporate it into your growth plan. Recognize and acknowledge your fear of criticism, and understand that feedback is meant to help you improve, not to criticize you personally. If the feedback is constructive, it shows that the person giving it cares about you and wants you to succeed.

Even if feedback feels negative, identify the helpful concepts within it. Studies show positive aspects can be derived despite initial negative feelings or the source of the feedback. Acknowledge what you are doing well and build on those aspects. If unsure about the feedback's meaning or application, ask for clarification to use it effectively. Finally, take action on the feedback to improve your skills and behaviors. As you apply it and experience growth, your fear of receiving feedback will diminish. And, collaboration has been shown to be 80% effective in solving problems or achieving objectives.

Fear of Rejection

Another common fear is the fear of rejection, where people worry that asking for feedback will make them seem weak or incompetent. To overcome this fear, remember that seeking feedback is a sign of strength and commitment to growth. Reframe the situation as an opportunity to improve rather than a personal indictment. Acknowledge this fear to your coach, communicate your concerns about appearing incompetent, and ask for feedback to identify areas for improvement while reassuring yourself that you are not incompetent.

It's essential to practice self-compassion and remember that everyone makes mistakes, which are a crucial part of the learning process. Embracing a growth mindset focused on learning and development, rather than perfection, will help you feel more confident and less anxious about making mistakes or being rejected. This approach will enable you to handle feedback more effectively and reduce fear over time.

Fear of Failure

Some people avoid seeking feedback due to a fear of failure, worrying it will confirm their worst fears. Remember, failure is a natural part of learning, and everyone has areas for improvement. Embrace failure as an opportunity for growth and use feedback to develop new strategies. Reframe failure as a learning opportunity, much like Edison did with his 2000+ attempts to invent the light bulb. Set realistic goals to reduce pressure and anxiety, with your coach helping to determine what is achievable.

Celebrate small successes to build confidence and momentum, as Bill Phillips advises: "Focus on progress, not perfection." Reflect on failures to learn and improve, identifying what went wrong and what to do differently next time. Seeking support from others, particularly a coach, can provide encouragement and guidance, helping you navigate challenges and setbacks effectively.

Fear of Change

Some people avoid seeking feedback because they fear being forced to make uncomfortable changes. If this resonates with you, remember that change is essential for growth and improvement. Focus on the benefits of the changes and find ways to make them manageable and achievable. If you have hired a coach, ask them to help you assess your current situation and identify what's not working, using your assessment results for insight. Recognize that change can bring significant benefits like personal growth, career advancement, and better relationships.

Work with your coach, mentor, or a willing friend to identify specific changes and create a plan to implement them. Taking control of the situation can reduce your fear of the unknown and empower you. This approach will help you navigate changes, stay motivated, and build confidence, making it easier to meet the challenges that come with change.

The Emotional-Physical Connection

For many people, the four fears we just discussed are strong and powerful emotions. Emotions can cause anyone to make rash decisions. Research shows that any time emotional stress is present in a situation, a few things happen in our physical bodies: adrenalin levels increase, the heartbeat is elevated, and cognitive capacity is decreased—you may have heard this referred to as the "fight or flight syndrome." If your heartbeat is elevated by 30%, you will have 30% less ability to reason and that doesn't usually produce a beneficial result. So, take a deep breath and try to revisit the issue when you can be more objective.

Constructive feedback can also come from mentors, colleagues, coaches, and even those you may not like but who possess relevant experience. Approach feedback with a willingness to learn, be specific about what you want to hear, and thank those who provide it, even if you don't agree with it. This demonstrates that you value their opinion and are open to their input, fostering a learning and improvement mindset.

While feedback is essential, self-reflection is equally important for gaining valuable insights and personal growth. Without self-reflection, you may miss understanding your thoughts, emotions, and behaviors deeply. This can be particularly challenging for introverts with lower motivation scores on the Coachability Index and strong extroverts who move quickly and miss subtle cues. Choosing the right coach, one whose behavior and mindset align with yours, is crucial for balancing feedback and self-reflection. Coaches vary in their approach, and finding one that makes you comfortable sharing your thoughts and feelings is important.

Self-reflection requires bravery to objectively evaluate your thoughts, feelings, and behaviors, which can be daunting. Balancing your communication style with your coach's approach is essential for effective feedback and self-reflection. The Coachability Index, discussed in Chapter 3, measures your drive to seek feedback and is particularly relevant for self-reflection, helping you identify blind spots and areas for improvement.

A lack of self-reflection can hinder your ability to recognize patterns, obstacles, or areas for improvement, limiting self-awareness and informed decision-making. This can be gleaned from journaling, meditating, or thinking about past experiences. Self-reflection allows you to dig deeper into your thoughts, feelings, and motivations, helping you identify areas for improvement. Choose specific, impactful experiences to reflect on, as these can reveal your strengths and areas needing improvement, aiding in setting realistic goals and developing plans for growth.

Be honest and patient with yourself, as self-discovery is a gradual process. Continuous reflection helps you identify what you want to achieve and how to achieve it. By focusing on significant experiences, you learn from your mistakes and make better decisions, leading to a more fulfilling life.

Balancing Feedback and Self-Reflection

Finding a balance between feedback and self-reflection requires intentionality and critical evaluation. Over-reliance on others' opinions can diminish self-awareness and personal growth, especially if the feedback is not constructive or accurate. Practicing the art of filtering useful feedback from unhelpful or biased comments is essential. This involves evaluating the source, considering multiple perspectives, and focusing on constructive criticism. Maintaining objectivity requires honest introspection and a willingness to acknowledge personal flaws and areas for improvement, ensuring you incorporate valuable feedback while staying true to your authentic self.

Managing emotions effectively when receiving feedback is crucial to prevent them from clouding your judgment or hindering self-reflection. Developing emotional intelligence and self-regulation skills can help navigate these emotional aspects, especially during frequent coaching sessions. Balancing feedback with self-reflection is key, as continuous feedback without time for reflection can be overwhelming, while excessive self-reflection without external input may limit growth. Striking the right balance enables meaningful self-assessment and broadens your perspective, facilitating personal and professional development.

Focusing on growth helps you adopt a mindset where feedback and self-reflection are seen as opportunities for improvement rather than criticism. This growth mindset is essential in a rapidly changing world, allowing you to adapt and meet new challenges. Seeking feedback and reflecting on your performance maximizes your achievement potential and leverages the experience and expertise of others. Embracing growth helps you persevere through setbacks and failures, turning them into valuable learning experiences. Employers value individuals who demonstrate a growth mindset, as it showcases a willingness to learn and grow, increasing your competitiveness in the job market and chances of professional success. Taking action on feedback and self-reflection transforms them into tools for growth and development.

Key Insights

Overcoming your fears about feedback and balancing Self-Reflection is an essential part of becoming more coachable. Recognizing and addressing your fears can help you develop a more positive and proactive approach to feedback. Remember that feedback is an opportunity for growth and improvement, and not a personal attack. With enough practice, seeking feedback can become a natural and empowering part of your personal and professional development. By seeking feedback, reflecting on experiences, finding a balance, focusing on growth, and taking action, you can use feedback and self-reflection as a tool for learning and improvement. With practice and effort, you will learn to find a balance between feedback and self-reflection and achieve your full potential.

Case Study: Lily

Lily had dreams of starting her own business, but she was held back by a deep fear of criticism, rejection, failure, and change. Every time she thought about taking a step toward her goal, her mind was filled with doubt and anxiety, so she decided to hire a life coach. During our initial coaching session, I could see the magnitude of Lily's fears. She knew that in order to succeed, she had to confront her fears head-on. I challenged Lily with a series of steps to gradually build her confidence and resilience.

The first challenge was to face her fear of criticism by sharing her business ideas with trusted friends and mentors. While apprehensive, she began to gain confidence upon receiving valuable insights to improve her ideas. I continued to push her boundaries by encouraging her to attend networking events and industry conferences. Although Lily faced rejections along the way, I continued to remind her that every "no" was simply a step closer to a "yes," which made her more resilient. Soon she started viewing rejection as an opportunity for growth.

Next, Lily tackled her fear of failure by recognizing that failures were actually learning experiences versus personal setbacks. She did that by relating to similar situations from her past experiences. We then set small, achievable goals and began celebrating each milestone, regardless of the outcome. Finally, we emphasized the importance of adaptability as I encouraged Lily to embrace change as an opportunity for growth by exploring new ideas, learning new skills, and taking calculated risks. Each time Lily stepped out of her comfort zone, she discovered new strengths and capabilities within herself.

As weeks turned into months, Lily transformed before my eyes. With each challenge she conquered, her confidence grew stronger. Lily eventually launched her own business—a unique blend of her passion and expertise. Although the road ahead was not without challenges, Lily's newfound courage and resilience allowed her to navigate them with grace and determination.

Reflection Questions:

1. Have you ever received feedback that was difficult to hear? How did you respond?

2. How can you respond to feedback in a more productive way?

3. How can you differentiate between feedback that is helpful and feedback that is unhelpful?

4. How can you use feedback to improve your relationships with others?

5. How and when can you make time for self-reflection in your daily life?

6. How can self-reflection improve your relationships with others?

7. What are some common mistakes people make when self-reflecting?

How can you practice overcoming these four types of fears about feedback?

1. Be kind and gentle with yourself and remind yourself that everyone experiences these fears at some point in their lives. When you notice negative self-talk or self-criticism, challenge it with positive affirmations and self-compassionate thoughts.

2. Begin by taking small steps toward the things that make you feel uncomfortable. For example, if you're afraid of criticism, share something with a trusted friend or family member and ask for feedback.

3. Try to reframe your thoughts about criticism, rejection, failure, and change. Instead of seeing them as negative experiences, view them as opportunities for growth and learning.

4. Embrace the idea that your abilities and skills can improve through past experiences, effort, and practice.

5. Gradually expose yourself to the things that trigger your fears. For example, if you're afraid of rejection, try asking for a discount at a store or requesting a small favor from someone.

6. Surround yourself with supportive people who encourage and motivate you—especially people who know you and your challenges well enough to be honest with you. Join a group or community where you can connect with others who share similar experiences and fears.

CHAPTER 6

Seeking Out the Right Coach or Mentor

Having a coach or mentor can be an invaluable resource for personal and professional growth. But how do you find the right coach or mentor? In this chapter, we'll explore some strategies for seeking out the right person to guide you on your journey.

Identify Your Goals

Setting goals is critical before choosing a coach because it helps you determine what kind of coaching you need and what type of coach is best suited to help you achieve those goals. When you have clear goals in mind, you can find a coach who specializes in the areas where you want to improve, and who has a track record of helping clients achieve similar goals.

Having clear goals also helps you evaluate the effectiveness of your coaching relationship. Keeping your eye on these goals can also help you stay motivated and focused throughout the coaching process. Having a sense of purpose and direction makes it easier for you to stay committed to the coaching process and overcome any obstacles that may arise along the way, including areas that may seem out of place or not as important to you as to your coach.

Initially, you will need to identify what you hope to achieve. What areas of your life or work do you want to improve? Ensure that all your goals are not just about getting rid of what you deem negative. Use your strengths to accelerate reaching your objectives. Depending on whether this is a short-term or long-term goal, you'll want to evaluate whether a professional coach or someone with another type of expertise will be best equipped to help you meet your objectives.

When you begin this process—especially if you have not worked with a coach in the past—remember that goal setting is a process. It may take some time to figure out what you want to achieve and how to get there with your strengths. Be patient with yourself and stay focused on your vision for the future.

Start by taking some time to reflect on what you really want that matters most to you. What do you really want to achieve? What are you passionate about, what brings you joy, and what do you want to improve in your life? Does it help you accomplish your purpose in life? If it does not, is the objective realistic and meaningful, long-term? Start with small goals in order to build momentum and confidence; consider setting short-term goals that are achievable within a few weeks or months.

Next, write down your goals. This will help clarify your thoughts and make them more concrete AND between 33% and 42% more effective according to studies at Dominican University of California and FounderJar! Writing down your goals also makes it easier for your coach to track your progress and for you to hold yourself accountable. Then break them down into small manageable steps that will be less overwhelming and easier to achieve. Seeing your goals on paper will also help you identify any obstacles or challenges that you may need to overcome as you pursue them.

Once you have something to work with, share your goals with people who can provide constructive feedback and support. This can be a friend, family member, or someone whose experience or advice you trust—like a coach or mentor! Finally, plug your goals into a SMART format. The SMART framework is a popular goal-setting technique that stands for **Specific, Measurable, Achievable, Relevant, and Timely.** If you are unfamiliar with the SMART Goals concept, you might want to consider taking a short course offered at this website: (https://www.lifethrive.com/ smart-approach-reaching-goals-objectives/) Once you are familiar with the process, you can apply it immediately.

Scan here!

Look for Compatibility

If you are new or still considering the coaching process, it's important to find a coach or mentor who is compatible with your personality, values, and communication style. Look for someone you feel comfortable talking to; it should also be a person you trust to give you honest feedback. As you are evaluating candidates, also consider factors such as age, gender, cultural background, general availability, or other factors that could impact your relationship.

On the other hand, if you have previously been through the coaching process and want to be stretched, you may seek out someone who is accomplished or skilled in areas where you lack experiential depth. You may also want to consider someone who has a different approach and sees things differently. That will stretch you but also require you to develop a deeper understanding of your own strengths and weaknesses. However, if you are just getting started with coaching, working with someone who is too "stretching" could end up being extremely stressful and, in many cases, counterproductive to your objectives.

When you and your coach have similar personalities, values, and communication styles, it becomes easier to establish a rapport and trust between you. If you are not comfortable opening up or sharing your personal and professional challenges with your coach, the coach will be less understanding of your perspective and the unique challenges you face. Building a solid foundation of understanding with your coach leads to a more targeted and personalized experience that is tailored to your needs.

Most importantly, when you and your coach have a good rapport and the coaching is personalized, it leads to better outcomes. You are more likely to engage in the coaching process, take ownership of your development, and achieve your desired goals.

Seek Referrals

Ask friends, colleagues, and acquaintances if they know of any coaches or mentors who may be a good fit for you. You can also seek recommendations from professional associations, industry groups, or online communities. Talk to multiple coaches before making a decision. You may even want to talk with some more than once. Rarely do you get the full picture the first time!

Referrals from people you know, and trust will normally be more valuable than anonymous reviews or online searches. You can ask them about their experience with a coach and get honest feedback about what worked well for them and what didn't. This will save you time in researching and vetting coaches. Referrals help you narrow down your search by sharing insights that could be helpful for you to know about a potential coach.

Additionally, referrals give you a better understanding of what to expect from the coaching process. Experienced coaches should provide insight into how coaching works, what the coach's role is, and what kind of results you might expect. So, referrals help you better identify a coach who matches your needs and personality. Friends, colleagues, or acquaintances may know you well enough to recommend a coach who has the approach, communication style, or expertise that you need.

Do Your Research

Once you've identified potential coaches or mentors, do your research. Look up their credentials, read reviews or testimonials, and check out their website or social media profiles. This will give you a sense of the coach's expertise, style, or approach.

Your research will help you ensure that the coach is a qualified and experienced professional whose expertise or approach will help you achieve your goals. Doing your research will help you select a qualified and experienced professional who has received proper training or certifications in coaching. It gives you, the client, confidence that you are working with someone whose knowledge and skills can support you in achieving your goals.

Schedule a Meeting

After vetting multiple coaches and before committing to a particular coach or mentor, schedule a casual meeting to get to know them better. This can be a phone call or video chat, but in most cases, an in-person meeting provides the best insight. Use this time to ask questions, discuss your goals, and get a sense of their coaching or mentoring style.

Here are some potential questions you might want to ask during your meeting:

1. What is your coaching experience and training?

2. What is your coaching style and approach?

3. Can you tell me about a coaching success story you've had with a similar client or situation?

4. How do you typically structure coaching sessions?

5. What are your expectations of me as a client?

6. How will we measure progress towards my goals?

7. What are your fees and what is included in those fees?

8. What are your policies around scheduling, rescheduling, or canceling sessions?

9. How often will we meet, and for how long?

10. Can you provide references from past clients?

Establish Expectations

Once you've found the right coach or mentor, it's time to establish expectations for the relationship. This includes setting goals, outlining the coaching or mentoring process, and discussing any fees or payment arrangements. Clear communication and mutual understanding are key to a successful coaching relationship. After all, coaching is designed to be a collaborative relationship.

Start by being clear about what you hope to achieve through coaching. Identify the areas you want to improve upon and be specific about what you hope to accomplish. It's important to communicate your expectations to your coach upfront: your goals, the areas you want to work on, and what you hope to gain from the coaching relationship.

Don't be afraid to ask your coach questions about their coaching style, approach, and experience. Understanding their background and how they work will help you set expectations that align with your needs. You should also be clear about how often you want to meet with your coach, and for how long. Establishing a regular meeting schedule will help you stay on track and ensure that you are making progress toward your goals. Last but not least, make sure you discuss issues of confidentiality and how your coach protects the private information of their clients.

Your Checklist For Evaluating Potential Coaches and Mentors

In this section, I have provided you with a sample checklist and reasoning behind the selection of a coach or mentor. If you follow these guidelines you should have a successful experience:

1. **Credentials and Experience:**
   - **Qualifications:** Verify the coach's certifications and educational background in coaching or related fields .
   - **Experience:** Look for a track record of successfully coaching individuals in your area of interest. Experienced coaches are often more adept at handling a variety of situations.

2. **Coaching Style and Approach:**
   - **Methodology:** Understand the coach's preferred coaching methods (e.g., cognitive-behavioral, solution-focused) and ensure they align with your learning style and goals.
   - **Flexibility:** Assess whether the coach is adaptable and can tailor their approach to fit your unique needs and circumstances.

3. **Communication Skills:**
   - **Active Listening:** Check if the coach practices active listening, demonstrating empathy and understanding of your concerns.
   - **Feedback:** Evaluate the clarity, constructiveness, and frequency of the feedback they provide. Effective coaches offer actionable insights without being overly critical.

4. Track Record and Testimonials:
- **Client Success Stories:** Request case studies or testimonials from previous clients to gauge the coach's effectiveness and impact.
- **Referrals:** Ask for referrals and speak directly with past clients to get a firsthand account of their coaching experience.

5. Ethical Standards and Professionalism:
- **Ethical Guidelines:** Ensure the coach adheres to professional ethical standards and guidelines, such as those outlined by the International Coach Federation (ICF).
- **Confidentiality:** Verify that the coach maintains strict confidentiality regarding your sessions and personal information.

6. Goal Alignment and Personal Fit:
- **Goal Setting:** Assess the coach's ability to help you set clear, achievable goals and create a structured plan to reach them.
- **Personal Fit:** Determine if there is a good personal fit between you and the coach, as a strong rapport can significantly enhance the coaching relationship.

7. Progress Tracking and Accountability:
- **Monitoring Progress:** Check how the coach tracks your progress and measures success. They should have a clear system for monitoring improvements and setbacks.

- **Accountability:** Evaluate the coach's ability to hold you accountable for your commitments and actions towards achieving your goals.

8. **Availability and Accessibility:**
   - **Session Frequency:** Confirm the frequency and duration of coaching sessions to ensure they meet your needs.
   - **Support Availability:** Understand the availability of the coach for support outside of scheduled sessions, including responsiveness to emails or calls.

Key Insights

Finding the right coach or mentor can be a game-changer for personal and professional growth. By identifying your goals, seeking referrals and doing your research, you can find someone who is a great match for your personality, values, and goals. With the right guidance and support, you can achieve your full potential and reach your goals.

Case Study: Sarah

A number of years ago, one of my instructors had a talented young student named Sarah. She had dreams of becoming an Olympic Taekwondo competitor and was willing to put in the hard work and dedication required to achieve her goals. She also had full support from her parents. Sarah approached one of our instructors to see if they could help her reach her full potential. Unfortunately, none of them were in a position to devote 2 – 4 hours a day to help her prepare for regional championships. Impatient and eager to start her training, she made a hasty decision and chose a coach who had achieved personal success, but only possessed limited coaching experience. Unfortunately, he committed to giving her more time than he really had available in his schedule.

Sarah's chosen coach, Coach Johnson, seemed promising at first. He had won numerous regional and national championships and possessed a reputable background, claiming to have trained successful athletes in the past. However, what Sarah failed to realize was that Coach Johnson's methods were outdated and ineffective for her specific needs. He lacked the ability to adapt to Sarah's unique sparring style and failed to provide her with the necessary conditioning, guidance, and support.

When Sarah barely won her match in regional competition, she started to notice the negative effects of her impulsive decision. Coach Johnson's outdated techniques hindered her progress instead of enhancing it. Her performance in the ring declined, and her confidence took a hit. Sarah realized that she had chosen the wrong coach in her haste to start training and achieve success.

Despite realizing her mistake, Sarah knew that it was important to learn from her experience. She made the difficult decision to part ways with Coach Johnson and take the time to find a coach who would commit the time necessary to help her reach her full potential. While the path to finding the right coach would be longer than she initially anticipated, Sarah remained determined to choose wisely this time and not let impatience cloud her judgment again.

Reflection Questions:

1. What are the 1-2 personality characteristics that you want to see in a coach or mentor?

2. How can you find a coach or mentor who shares your values?

3. What are the areas of expertise that would make a coach or mentor a good fit to help you achieve your goals?

4. What are some common mistakes people make when seeking out a coach or mentor?

5. How can you make the most of your time with your coach or mentor?

How can you take the steps necessary to find the right coach?

1. Don't skip any of the steps outlined in this chapter.

2. If you have doubts, ask someone who knows you well to interview the potential coach.

3. Speak to his or her former clients.

4. Does this coach "feel" right to you? (Pay attention to your "gut" instincts.)

5. Make sure there is a comfort level with the coach.

CHAPTER 7

Embracing a Growth Mindset

Having a growth mindset is essential to being coachable. Stanford professor Carol Dweck in her book Mindset, describes people with a growth mindset are the ones who feel their skills and intelligence can be improved with effort and persistence. That characteristic allows you to approach learning and development with a positive attitude and a willingness to improve. A growth mindset is a belief that one's abilities and intelligence can be developed through dedication and hard work, and that failures and setbacks are opportunities for growth and learning.

The more you embrace a growth mindset, the higher your score in the "Motivation" area of the LifeThrive Coachability Index will be. The reason for this is simple: as you start to understand that growth can occur regardless of how perfectly you perform, you will be more motivated to keep moving forward.

If you have a growth mindset, you are open to feedback and willing to make changes in your perspective on how things ought to be done, even if you do so reluctantly. You are not afraid to take risks and try new things, even if it means making mistakes along the way. This mindset allows you to see challenges as opportunities to learn and grow, rather than as threats to your self-esteem or competence. It also allows you to maintain a positive attitude toward your own development and growth over time.

Being coachable means being receptive to feedback and guidance from others—even if the feedback isn't coming from your favorite person! This critical measurement on the Coachability Index helps both you and your coach identify if it may be challenging for you to accept feedback and/or embrace it during the growth process. Someone with a fixed mindset may feel defensive or resistant to feedback, seeing it as a reflection of their innate abilities or flaws. On the other hand, having a growth mindset makes you more likely to view feedback as a way to improve and develop your skills. In this chapter, you'll learn more about what it means to have a growth mindset and how to develop one.

Focus on Effort, Not Talent

One of the key aspects of a growth mindset is the focus on effort rather than innate talent. Instead of thinking, "I'm not good at this," tell yourself: "I can improve with practice and effort." This shifts the emphasis from your present fixed traits to the potential for growth and development.

While talent is often seen as an innate ability, effort is something that you can control. By focusing on effort, you are more likely to put in the time and energy to develop the skills and abilities needed to improve. This leads to greater progress and success in the long run. Developing a growth mindset through your effort can help you bounce back from setbacks and failures—and this resilience is an important trait for success in any field.

Additionally, when you focus on effort, you develop a curiosity and love of learning that can help you stay motivated and engaged in the coaching process. It helps you continue to grow and develop over time. Studies have shown that effort is a better predictor of success than talent. For example, research by Angela Duckworth and Martin Seligman found that grit, or the combination of passion and perseverance, was a better predictor of success in West Point cadets than IQ.[3] Similarly, a study by David Conley and William E. Condon found that effort was a better predictor of college success than SAT scores.[4] Clearly, effort leads to the development of skills and abilities that are necessary for success, while talent alone is not enough.

To further illustrate this point, think about how much effort goes into learning a new skill or concept. In the Overview section of this book, you may recall reading about Hermann Ebbinghaus and his pioneering research on the "forgetting curve" as well as the learning curve. But here's another interesting fact about learning: a study conducted by John Dunlosky and his colleagues at Kent State University found that students who studied a concept *six times* performed significantly better on a test than students who studied the concept only once.[5] Making the effort to internalize new information through repetition can help you build the resil-

3   Duckworth & Seligman, "Grit: Perseverance and Passion for Long-Term Goals" (2007). *Journal of Personality and Social Psychology*.

4   Conley & Condon, "College Knowledge: What It Takes for Students to Succeed and What Colleges Can Do to Help" (2009). Published by the *American College Testing (ACT)* organization.

5   Dunlosky et al., "Improving Students' Learning with Effective Learning Techniques: Promising Directions from Cognitive and Educational Psychology" (2013). *Psychological Science in the Public Interest*.

ience necessary to push past your present knowledge into deeper understanding.

Embrace Challenges

People with a growth mindset embrace challenges as opportunities for growth and learning. When you face a challenge, you are forced to step out of your comfort zone and take risks, which can help you learn new things about yourself and the world around you. Instead of avoiding difficult tasks, you can view them as a chance to learn and improve.

Challenges can be difficult. There's no way around that. But embracing them helps you develop resilience, which is the ability to bounce back from setbacks. Persevering through a challenge teaches you to develop your growth mindset and deepen your character—and people with character address and overcome obstacles with hope and an expectation of success.

Challenges also force you to think outside of the box and come up with creative solutions. When faced with a difficult problem, you may need to explore different approaches and perspectives in order to develop new ideas and insights. When those insights help you overcome the challenge, you gain a sense of accomplishment that helps you tackle future challenges with more confidence and motivation.

Being coachable allows you to embrace new challenges so you can grow and gain knowledge from new experiences. Pushing yourself outside of your comfort zone may help you discover new interests or passions or learn new skills that you can apply to other areas of your life.

Seek Out Feedback

People with a growth mindset actively seek out feedback and use it to improve. Don't be afraid of criticism; instead, view feedback as a valuable tool for growth and development. By listening to feedback and incorporating it into your growth plan, you'll continue to improve and achieve your goals. Seeking feedback from your coach will give you a greater chance of keeping life's challenges in perspective.

A study by Cutumisu, Lou, and Noels (2020) found that students with a growth mindset were more likely to seek feedback from their teachers than students with a fixed mindset. The students with a growth mindset also benefited more from the feedback they received. They were more likely to use the feedback to improve their performance on subsequent tasks.

Another study by Papi, Bondarenko, Wawire, Jiang, and Zhou (2019) found that students with a growth mindset were more likely to seek feedback from their peers. The students with a growth mindset also perceived the feedback they received from their peers to be more helpful than the students with a fixed mindset.

These studies suggest that people with a growth mindset are more likely to seek feedback from others to improve their skills and knowledge. Feedback can provide valuable information about how to improve, and people with a growth mindset are more likely to use this information to their advantage.

Learn from Mistakes

When you reflect on mistakes and identify areas for improvement, you can develop new strategies and approaches for success. After all, making mistakes is a natural part of life's learning process, and it helps individuals develop new skills and knowledge. Your coach can help you reframe the challenges or mistakes you encounter as steps forward in your journey.

Viewing mistakes as a sign of failure can lead to negative emotions, such as shame or guilt, which inhibit your learning and growth capacity. However, when you view mistakes as an opportunity to learn, it leads to increased self-awareness, improved problem-solving skills, and a greater willingness to take risks and try new things. Think about it this way: "There is no such thing as failure. I either succeed or learn from my mistakes."

In reality, mistakes are often the result of trying something new or challenging oneself—which is a positive thing in and of itself. Think about it this way: A mother realizes that her child is going to make mistakes but continues her love for the child. When the child makes a mistake, the mother helps the child learn how to correct the error quickly while it is still fresh on the child's mind. As an adult, you learn that it is proper to address your mistake, try to fix it if possible, and move on!

Develop a Curious Mind

People with a growth mindset are curious about the world around them and are eager to learn new things. When you approach new experiences with an open mind and a desire to learn, it develops your intellectual curiosity and lifelong love of learning. Keep asking questions, seeking new information, and building curiosity as you explore new areas and ideas. Those characteristics can expand your understanding of the world and open up new opportunities for growth and development.

On the other hand, a fixed mindset is characterized by a belief that abilities and intelligence are predetermined and cannot be changed. Individuals with a fixed mindset tend to avoid challenges, give up easily when faced with obstacles, and view failure as a sign of their own limitations. This can lead to a stagnant and unfulfilling life—and who wants that?

In contrast, remember that a growth mindset is characterized by a belief that abilities and intelligence can be developed through hard work and persistence. So, choose to embrace challenges, persist in the face of obstacles, and view failure as an opportunity to learn and grow! Staying curious will lead you to a more fulfilling, satisfying life with greater success and happiness.

Celebrate Progress

You learned in a previous chapter that when progress occurs, sharing it reinforces that progress. People with a growth mindset celebrate progress, no matter how small. By recognizing and celebrating your achievements, you can stay motivated and focused on your goals—and this reinforces the idea that hard work and effort can lead to positive outcomes. When you celebrate your achievements, especially with friends or colleagues, both you and your friends remind yourself that your efforts have paid off. These multiple sources can motivate and encourage you to continue working toward your goals.

Celebrating progress also provides a healthy boost to your confidence and self-esteem, regardless of whether you can do so with others or not. Recognizing your achievements can help you maintain an attitude of optimism, even in the face of setbacks or failures. Focus on what's working and what you've accomplished, rather than dwelling on what's not working or what you haven't yet achieved.

Finally, celebrating successes is a great way to overcome a fixed mindset. People with a fixed mindset tend to believe that abilities and intelligence are fixed and cannot be changed. That's not true! Celebrating your successes, however large or small they may be, helps you recognize that your abilities and intelligence can improve and grow with effort and dedication. Trust in your ability to learn and improve and believe that you can achieve your goals through hard work and dedication.

Key Insights

Embracing a growth mindset is essential to being coachable and achieving personal and professional growth. Focusing on effort, embracing challenges, learning from mistakes, seeking out feedback, developing curiosity, and celebrating progress can help you develop a mindset that enables you to reach your full potential. With practice and effort, a growth mindset can become a natural and empowering part of your life.

Case Study: Abby

Abby was a strong-willed young lady. She believed that was just who she was, and that she could not change. This mindset was holding her back from realizing her objective of becoming an elementary school teacher. After sharing several studies and the concept of a growth mindset—the idea that intelligence and abilities are not fixed—we began to identify Abby's strengths and weaknesses. We then began to develop a SMART plan for her to go back to college and complete her degree.

Several years later, I ran into Abby in a grocery store. She shared with me that after accomplishing her SMART objectives, she began to believe that working hard and challenging herself to complete college could pay big dividends. She also started to seek feedback from others. She began to achieve her goals, and she developed a more positive self-image that boosted her confidence, which further led to graduating in the top 10% of her class.

Before we parted, Abby shared another success. One day, while working on a difficult project, she was struggling and about to give up. It reminded her of the concept of a growth mindset and that she just needed to keep working hard. She was not only able to complete the project, but the success resulted in her being named teacher of the month at her school.

Reflection Questions:

1. What are some common misconceptions about a growth mindset?

2. How can a growth mindset help you learn from failure?

3. What is the relationship between a growth mindset and resilience?

4. How can you maintain a growth mindset during challenging times?

5. What are some ways to cultivate a growth mindset in your daily life?

How will you know if you have taken the steps necessary to embrace a growth mindset?

1. You can define the differences between growth and fixed mindsets.

2. You no longer avoid challenges but see them as opportunities.

3. You are focusing on the process, not individual outcomes.

4. You are seeking supportive and encouraging people to inspire you.

5. You are cultivating a love of learning.

CHAPTER 8

The Power of Positivity and Resilience

Self-talk refers to the internal dialogue or the messages that individuals give themselves, consciously or unconsciously, which can influence their emotions, beliefs, and actions. Did you know that your inner dialogue can greatly impact your ability to be coachable? Positive self-talk is a powerful tool that has a significant impact on both your behavior and mindset. It can help you overcome obstacles, build resilience, and achieve your goals. In this chapter, we'll discuss how to develop positive self-talk and use it to achieve success.

Becoming aware of your self-talk patterns is an important step in becoming more coachable. The more positives you introduce into your life, the higher the likelihood that positive outcomes will grow out of you. Allowing others to give you feedback can help you replace negative or limiting self-talk with positive and empowering self-talk. Your coach can support you in this phase of developing a growth mindset and focusing on your goals.

Recognize Negative Self-Talk

Before you can become a master of positive self-talk, you'll first need to start recognizing the opposite. This includes negative thoughts, limiting beliefs, and self-criticism. To become more coachable, you must learn to challenge the negative self-talk and replace it with positive, empowering thoughts. Becoming familiar with some specific types of negative self-talk that inhibit growth and development can give you an advantage. Here are a few examples:

- Do you find that you are **constantly criticizing** and judging yourself? For example, do you tell yourself things like, "I'm not good enough" or "I always mess things up."
- Do you **imagine the worst possible outcomes** for a situation, even if the likelihood of that happening is low? For example, if you receive a negative comment at work, you may immediately assume that you are going to get fired.
- Do you see things in **"all-or-nothing"** terms, without any shades of gray? For example, if you make a mistake, you may think that you are a complete failure and that there is no coming back from it.
- Do you **take responsibility** for things that are beyond your control? For example, if a project at work fails, you may blame yourself for not doing enough, even if there were other factors at play.
- Do you **apply one negative experience** to everything else? For example, if you fail an exam, you

may assume that you are not smart enough for school in general.

By becoming aware of these patterns, you can start to challenge and reframe your thoughts to be more positive and empowering. A coach can also help you identify and work through negative self-talk patterns in a supportive and constructive way.

Practice Gratitude

Gratitude is an important part of positive self-talk. By focusing on what you're grateful for, you can shift our perspective from focusing on what's lacking or what's going wrong in your life to what is going well. Practicing gratitude in your self-talk can help you reframe your thoughts to be more positive and optimistic, which improves your overall well-being and quality of life. The resulting sense of optimism and hope can be essential fuel for achieving your goals.

When you express gratitude, you activate the brain's neuro-plasticity and reward system to release neurotransmitters like dopamine and serotonin, which can help you feel happier, more content, and less stressed. This has a ripple effect on your mood, relationships, and productivity—effectively bringing about more positive outcomes in various areas of your life. Additionally, gratitude helps you develop resilience and emotional intelligence as you learn to appreciate the good things in life—even in the face of challenges and setbacks. By incorporating gratitude into your self-talk, you can cultivate a more positive and resilient mindset to help you navigate life's ups and downs with greater ease and grace. As you develop an "attitude of gratitude," you will see changes in your perspective, outlook, and relationships.

Use Affirmations

Affirmations are positive statements that you repeat to yourself to reinforce positive beliefs and attitudes. Affirmations are helpful because they can change the way you think and feel about yourself and your life.

By using affirmations regularly, you can develop a more positive self-image and build confidence. Your beliefs and attitudes shape your thoughts and actions, and often those beliefs are influenced by the experiences and people around you. Affirmations can help counteract these negative beliefs by focusing on positive thoughts and feelings. By repeating positive affirmations to yourself, you can start to shift your beliefs and attitudes toward a more positive outlook. For example, if you repeat the affirmation "I am capable and successful" to yourself regularly, you should begin to believe in your own unique and God-given abilities and become more proactive about achieving your goals.

Set Realistic Goals

Multiple times in the preceding chapters you have read about the need for setting realistic goals because without them, the coaching process can become frustrating for both parties. A competent coach understands that this is essential to building resilience. However, sometimes you may find that the objectives you and your coach set are *not* realistically attainable under your present circumstances. "Life gets in the way" sometimes and we have to be flexible enough to recognize these curves in the road, slow down, and readjust.

Many people need a strong support system in place to help them succeed. You must have the support of family, friends, or colleagues who can step in and help you during the challenging stages of the process. Not only do you need encouragement from your coach, but in order to progress, you may also need their input to identify if the objective is out of reach or adjustments need to be made. This is why we suggest the need for a strong support system as there will be times when the coach is simply not available to you.

Your coach should be able to provide the wise counsel and recommendations necessary to help you along the way. If they do not, you may want to seek the advice of others who may have more experience or expertise in your focus area.

Then Visualize Success

Visualization is a powerful tool for developing confidence and motivation because it activates the same neural pathways in the brain as actual experiences do. This means that when you visualize yourself successfully achieving your goals, your brain reacts as if you actually achieved those goals! Many Olympic athletes have used visualization as a highly effective tool to achieve success beyond what they might accomplish through normal workouts alone.

Additionally, visualization can help you overcome negative thought patterns and self-doubt. By visualizing yourself succeeding and feeling confident, you can begin to reframe unhelpful thoughts and beliefs about yourself and enjoy a higher level of self-esteem and confidence. Visualization helps you create a clear mental picture or roadmap of what you want to achieve and what steps are needed to get there. Having that roadmap provides direction and the steps necessary for achieving your goals. That in and of itself can be extremely motivating.

Develop Coping Strategies

A coach can help you develop coping strategies for dealing with setbacks and challenges. This can include developing a support network, practicing self-care, and reframing negative thoughts. With coping strategies in place, you can build resilience and overcome obstacles more easily.

When working toward an important objective, you will often face challenges, discouragement, or problems that can seem overwhelming. The first thing you may want to consider is taking time to step back and take care of yourself. Go for a walk, read a book, or do something else that you enjoy. While it may appear to slow down your progress, you must learn to be kind to yourself while acknowledging that setbacks happen to everyone. A wise man once said this: "Sometimes you have to slow down to speed up." And that is so very true!

Think about people like George Eastman, the inventor of the Kodak camera. He failed at several businesses before he finally found success with Kodak. Then there was Alexander Graham Bell, the inventor of the telephone. He failed at several other inventions before he finally succeeded with the telephone. And what about The Wright Brothers? While they are credited with inventing the airplane, they failed at multiple attempts to fly before they finally succeeded. Tuck this thought away: **"Failure is success, if you learn from it."**

Additionally, you might also want to seek outside support from friends, family, or even a therapist. Talking to others can help you process your emotions, gain perspective on the situation, and will help you maintain a positive outlook by reminding you of the things that are going well. With an attitude of gratitude, you will be able to take the next steps toward your goal, even if things are not perfect. Incorporating that positivity can help you regain a sense of control and momentum.

Celebrate Progress

You may be getting tired of hearing this, but a coach and/or your support system can help you celebrate progress, no matter how small. By recognizing and celebrating achievements, you can build motivation and momentum. The resulting self-efficacy and confidence are both essential components of resilience.

Celebrating progress is critical to maintaining motivation during the coaching process. When you do not acknowledge your progress, it can lead to discouragement. When you feel that your efforts are not enough, it deflates your confidence and self-esteem, and may cause you to lose the enthusiasm to continue working toward your objectives.

Additionally, demotivation may turn to burnout, which leads to decreased productivity, a loss of interest in the goal, and even physical and emotional exhaustion. When progress is not celebrated, you can quickly forget or discount the accomplishments made toward your goal. Don't overlook the progress you have made and focus solely on what is left to be achieved! This can only lead to feelings of frustration and discouragement.

Surround Yourself with Positive Influences

Your environment can greatly impact your self-talk. By surrounding yourself with positive influences in addition to your coach, such as supportive friends and colleagues, you can reinforce positive beliefs and attitudes to a greater extent. Building a positive community around you can make it easier to stay motivated and focused on your goals.

For starters, positive influences provide encouragement and support. When you see others achieving success and making progress toward their goals, it inspires you to do the same. When the people around you believe in you and your abilities, it can boost your confidence and give you the inspiration and motivation to keep working toward your goals.

Most importantly, positive influences can help you maintain a positive attitude and mindset. For those who are surrounded by negativity and pessimism, it can be difficult to stay motivated and focused on goals. However, surrounding yourself with positivity and optimism can help you maintain a positive outlook, even when faced with challenges.

Key Insights

Positive self-talk is a powerful tool that can help you achieve your goals and overcome obstacles. By recognizing negative self-talk, practicing gratitude, using affirmations, visualizing success, and surrounding yourself with positive influences, you can develop a more positive self-image and build confidence. With practice and effort, positive self-talk can become a natural and empowering part of your life.

Also, coaching can be a powerful tool for helping you build resilience. By developing a growth mindset, identifying strengths and weaknesses, setting realistic goals, developing coping strategies, and celebrating progress, you can build the resilience needed to overcome challenges and achieve success. With the right guidance and support, you will develop the resilience needed to succeed.

Case Study: Alex

When I first met Alex, I was concerned about his dismal outlook, deeply negative attitude, and constant self-doubt. He was convinced that life was never positive enough, productive enough, or good enough to meet his or his family's needs. His negative mindset affected his work, relationships, and overall happiness.

One day, Alex decided that enough was enough and sought my help as a life coach. My first step was to raise awareness about his negative thoughts and the impact those thoughts were having on virtually every aspect of his life. We began by helping him reframe his negative beliefs to develop an attitude of gratitude, which was indeed a challenge because of his long history of negativity.

Each time he visited, he was required to bring a list of what he had been grateful for since his last visit. Together, we started practicing gratitude exercises, focusing on the positive aspects of his life, and acknowledging the things he was thankful for. As Alex shifted his attention toward gratitude, he began to experience a shift in their perspective. It wasn't long before he realized that despite his flaws and challenges, he had many reasons to be grateful.

Next, I required that he verbalize positive affirmations into our meetings and then into his daily routine. Every morning he would repeat the phrase: "I am capable and deserving of success." Over time, these affirmations started to replace the negative self-talk, building a foundation of self-belief and confidence which helped him visualize his success and create a SMART plan to develop his goals and dreams.

Alex began to set small, attainable goals and celebrated each milestone along the way. The more he affirmed his capacity and visualized a different way of life, I could see his motivation and focus changing his whole paradigm of thought.

> Within a year, he was ready to start surrounding himself with positive influences other than myself. With his newfound confidence, Alex sought out supportive friends, inspiring mentors, and uplifting resources. Alex joined a community of like-minded individuals who shared their aspirations and supported one another's growth. Alex no longer needed my help!

Reflection Questions:

1. How can positive self-talk help you be more coachable?

2. In what ways can positive self-talk help you stay motivated?

3. What are some examples of positive self-talk?

4. How can you make positive self-talk a habit?

5. How can positive self-talk improve your relationships with others?

6. What are some common traits of resilient people?

7. How can resilience improve your mental health?

8. What role does self-awareness play in building resilience?

Have you taken the steps necessary to embrace positive self-talk and increase resilience?

1. Can you reframe a negative thought into a positive one?

2. When you catch yourself engaging in negative self-talk, do you challenge those thoughts by asking if there is evidence to support those thoughts or if they are just assumptions?

3. Can you be kind and compassionate to yourself with the same kindness and understanding that you would show to a friend or loved one?

4. Have you created a list of positive affirmations that resonate with you and repeat them to yourself regularly?

5. Do you surround yourself with people who support and uplift you?

6. Have you identified how to interpret your strengths and weaknesses to help you develop attainable objectives?

7. Are you connected to others that can provide you with emotional support during difficult times?

8. Are you learning how to manage stress so you can cope with difficult situations and prevent burnout?

CHAPTER 9

OVERCOMING RESISTANCE TO CHANGE

Change can be difficult, but it's often necessary for personal and professional growth. Resistance to change is an obstacle that many people face, but there are strategies for overcoming it. In this chapter, we'll discuss common reasons people resist change and how to overcome them.

In 1927, H. P. Lovecraft theorized: "The oldest and strongest emotion of mankind is fear, and the oldest and strongest kind of fear is fear of the unknown." Not knowing what to expect can be scary because it means you lose control of your situation. You may be afraid of the new challenges, the uncertainty, or the consequences that change will bring. It can be scary when you can't plan for the future—whether it's because you fear losing a job, a relationship, or your sense of security.

When you are faced with change, you are forced to step outside of your comfort zone. This can be uncomfortable because it means learning new things and adapting to new ways of doing things. You may be afraid of failing at something new or being judged by others for not being able to keep up with the change.

To overcome this, it's important to gather information about the change and develop a plan for how to manage it. By understanding the change and having a plan in place, you can feel more prepared and less anxious. The more you know about the change, the less unknown it will be. Talk to people who have already gone through similar changes, read about this particular type of change, and watch videos about the change.

You should also consider talking to people about your fears because that can lead you to better understand the fears and to find ways to cope with them. Talk to friends, family, or a therapist—at least take some initial small steps to face the change. Don't try to change everything all at once. This will help you feel more in control and less overwhelmed.

Most importantly, be patient. Change takes time. Don't expect to feel comfortable with the change overnight; give yourself time to adjust. Remember, change is not always easy, but it is often necessary. If you can overcome your fear of the unknown, you will be better able to embrace change and grow as a person.

Fear of Failure: While we have focused on this concept in earlier chapters, remember that it will impact multiple aspects of your ability to grow. Fear of failure is a very common reason people resist change. To overcome this, you can reframe failure as a learning experience.

By recognizing that failure is an inevitable part of growth and development, you can become more open to taking risks and trying new things. Failure is a natural part of life. It happens to everyone. The important thing is to learn from your failures and use them to improve yourself. When you view failure as a learning opportunity, you are less likely to be afraid of it.

Failure is not the end of the world. Failure does not mean that YOU are a failure. It simply means that you did not succeed at something. There are many other opportunities out there. You can always try again. When you don't view failure as "the end of the world," you are less likely to be afraid of it. Consider this quote by Robert T. Klyosaki:

"Failure is part of the process of success. People who avoid failure also avoid success."

Consider adopting our previous quote of "failure is success if you learn from it!" Take the time to celebrate learning from mistakes. That's right, celebrate and remind yourself that "I won't be doing that again!" Be willing to ask others for help because then you will not be alone whether you succeed or fail. Success will rarely be attained on your own, nor will it be perfect on your first try.

Change also introduces perceived risks and drawbacks, especially if the benefits of the change are not immediately apparent. People tend to focus on potential drawbacks, such as increased workload, job insecurity, or disruption of interpersonal relationships, but one day will never be the same as the next. Consider this quote from Heraclitus: "The only thing that is constant is change." This focus on risks and potential negative outcomes can make you resistant to change, even if the change may ultimately benefit you.

One of the best ways to view change more positively is to educate yourself about the benefits of the change and try some small-scale experiments (trial and error) to reduce anxiety as the benefits of the change become more apparent. After all, change can force you to step outside of your comfort zone and learn new things. That mindset can lead to personal growth and development and create new opportunities for you. Additionally, you may be able to learn new skills, meet new people, or experience new things.

Comfort with the Status Quo: Organizations and people sometimes resist change simply because they're deeply ingrained in their culture. It's hard to give up the comfort of your familiar routines or established ways of doing things. Change often disrupts your routines, processes, systems, or ways of thinking, taking you out of your established comfort zones. To overcome this, focus on the benefits of the change and how it may enhance your personal or professional growth. By understanding the benefits of the change, you can become more motivated to embrace it.

Many people develop an emotional attachment to the status quo because there is a familiarity and predictability with existing systems, structures, or traditions. If you have invested time and effort into creating and maintaining that mindset, any proposed change might feel like a threat to your accomplishments or identity. This emotional attachment might tempt you to try and protect what you have built. Humans have a tendency to seek information that confirms their existing beliefs, while ignoring or rejecting information that challenges those beliefs. To overcome this tendency, you will need to be clear about your goals, be as transparent as possible about each step of the new approach, and be more patient with others as you face the upcoming change.

Lack of Control: You may resist change if you feel a situation is out of your control. This feeling can impede your decision-making, diminish your sense of ownership and accountability, limit your adaptability, reduce your motivation and engagement, and stifle your innovation and creativity. Getting involved in the change process can empower you to overcome these barriers and foster more productive outcomes.

One way to restore a sense of control is to identify areas where you are gifted, both behaviorally and in terms of your priorities in approaching change. For example, you may be better than most at multitasking and able to juggle more balls than the average person. Focusing on your strengths, rather than the change itself, can help you feel more empowered and less resistant to change. Remember, overcoming the lack of control during change is a gradual process. Be patient with yourself and allow yourself time to adjust and grow through the experience.

Finally, a lack of support from leaders, managers or team members can also create barriers that impede your participation in productive change efforts. Many times, team members do not understand what they are empowered or not empowered to do, especially if they do not see the objective as something that is feasible. An unsupportive or disengaged organizational or team culture can undermine the availability of resources, amplify resistance, limit access to expertise, as well as impact the mental health of some team members who do not completely understand their role in the change process.

Overcoming these hurdles may require you to cultivate support from various stakeholders in order to foster a positive environment and address the concerns associated with change. You should also be willing to seek out a support network of friends, family, colleagues, or a coach to help you feel more motivated and empowered to embrace change.

Key Insights

Overcoming resistance to change is essential to personal and professional growth. By understanding common reasons for resistance--such as fear of the unknown, fear of failure, comfort with the status quo, lack of control, and lack of support--you can develop strategies for overcoming it. With the right mindset and support, you can learn to embrace change and achieve your full potential.

Case Study: James

When James first came to me, he was already known for his exceptional skills in his field and was highly respected by his colleagues. However, deep down, he felt a growing sense of stagnation, yearning for something more—something that would push him out of his comfort zone and allow him to explore new possibilities. He hoped that by working with me he could overcome his resistance to change and possibly losing his "status."

He shared his aspirations and fears with me since I provided a safe space for him to express himself. However, he also recognized his fear of the unknown, fear of failure, aversion to risk, lack of control, and the lack of support in his present situation. I empathized with his concerns, acknowledging that change could be intimidating and that stepping into the unknown required courage.

Our first step was helping James identify his goals and envision the positive outcomes that awaited him on the other side of change. We focused on the importance of taking small steps and celebrating each milestone along the way while maintaining his present role. Gradually, James learned to view failure as an opportunity for growth instead of an obstacle. This reduced his fear of taking risks and allowed him to explore different strategies and possibilities. His research helped him find the tools that reduced the failure rates and outcomes, teaching him how to mitigate risks effectively. He gained a newfound confidence in his ability to navigate uncertainty.

Next, we focused on adapting and embracing flexibility by reframing his mindset and emphasizing the positive aspects of change. This was the catalyst James needed to begin building a new support network around him, which provided guidance and mentorship in his new areas of focus. Through networking events and industry conferences, James connected with like-minded individuals who became sources of inspiration and encouragement.

James gradually overcame his resistance. He started taking calculated risks, pursuing new opportunities, and stepping out of his comfort zone. Soon, James was flourishing and ready to move on. Most importantly, he became an advocate for change and an example for those who were resistant to expanding their horizons and opportunities. James's journey is a powerful reminder that with the right mindset, support, and coaching, anyone can overcome their resistance to change and unlock their full potential.

Reflection Questions:

1. Why do people resist change?

2. How can resistance to change hold you back?

3. How can you identify when you are resistant to change?

4. What are some steps you can take to embrace change?

5. How can a coach or mentor help you overcome resistance to change?

What are some steps you can take to overcome resistance to change during the coaching process?

1. While many circumstances are beyond your control, identify the elements that you can influence. Direct your energy and efforts towards those areas.

2. Take the initiative to gather information and learn as much as you can about the changes taking place. This will empower you to make informed decisions and feel more in control.

3. Cultivate flexibility in your thinking and approach. Be open to new ideas, perspectives, and solutions. This mindset allows you to adjust more readily to unexpected situations.

4. When faced with significant changes, break them down into smaller, manageable steps so the change is more controlled and less overwhelming.

5. Reflect on previous times when you've experienced change and consider how you successfully coped with them. Remind yourself of your resilience and ability to adapt.

CHAPTER 10

ACCOUNTABILITY AND FOLLOW-THROUGH

As you learned at the beginning of this book, the most challenging part of being held accountable by a coach is admitting that you need help. It can be difficult to admit that you are not perfect and that you need someone to help you achieve your goals. Just remember that everyone needs help sometimes, and a coach can be a valuable resource, especially if you have taken the time to ensure they are the right coach.

You also learned that being held accountable by a coach means being open to feedback, and that is why we measure it on the Coachability Index. It can be difficult to hear negative feedback but be assured that your coach's goal is to help you improve. Feedback can be a valuable tool for learning and growth, but only if you can stay accountable. Although it can be easy to slip back into old habits, remember why you are working with a coach in the first place. Stay focused on your goals and know that your coach is there to help you achieve them.

Accountability can also help you to identify and overcome obstacles. When you are struggling, the coach can help you identify the root of the problem and develop a plan to overcome it, leveraging their experience and facilitating conversations about your SMART goals. This can help you to move forward and achieve your goals more quickly and efficiently. Additionally, accountability builds trust and rapport between you and your coach. When you know that you can trust the coach to hold you accountable, you are more likely to be open and honest with the coach. A strong relationship with your coach is essential for a successful partnership.

Being coachable also requires follow-through. Accountability means taking responsibility for your actions and decisions, while follow-through means completing the commitments you made. In this chapter, we'll discuss how a coach can hold you accountable and help you follow through on commitments.

One way a coach could help you stay accountable is by **checking in regularly**: Meeting with your coach on a regular basis allows you to discuss your progress and to receive support and encouragement. However, there may be times when you need additional input or direction when preparing for a coaching session or when you are struggling with a specific goal or objective. Be sure to ask your coach how they want to handle these types of interactions—they may prefer that you contact them via email, by phone, or by scheduling a meeting through their online calendar.

Providing feedback: Your coach can provide feedback on your progress and offer suggestions for improvement. The coach will need to be specific about what you did well or what you could improve on. For example, he or she could say, "I really liked the way you handled that difficult customer" or "I noticed that you didn't make eye contact with the audience during your presentation." A good coach will also be constructive in the way they approach that feedback, avoiding personal attacks or criticism.

If you refer back to Chapter 4, you will remember that expressed humility is the most important factor for growth and development. Being humble doesn't mean you are a doormat; it means you realize that you don't have all the answers to every situation and circumstance. Your mind is built to take in, assimilate and apply new information in the prefrontal cortex.

The prefrontal cortex is a large area of the brain located at the front of the head. It is responsible for a variety of high-level cognitive functions, including planning, decision-making, and problem-solving. It is also involved in learning and memory. When you learn something new, the prefrontal cortex helps you to store the information in your long-term memory. It also helps you make connections between new information and existing knowledge so that you can use the new information to solve problems, make decisions, and plan for the future.

The prefrontal cortex is also involved in emotional regulation. When you experience strong emotions, the prefrontal cortex helps you control your emotions and respond in a way that is appropriate to the situation. This is important for learning, as it allows you to focus on the task at hand without being distracted by your emotions. The prefrontal cortex is a complex and dynamic part of the brain. It is constantly changing and adapting, which allows you to learn and grow throughout your life.

Next, as you will remember from previous chapters, we discussed the need for SMART goals. There is a body of research indicating that SMART goals are more effective than other goal-setting methods.

One study, conducted by Gail Matthews at Dominican University of California, found that people who set SMART goals were more likely to achieve their goals than those who did not. The study found that SMART goals were particularly effective for weight loss, exercise, and academic goals.[6]

Another study, conducted by Teresa Amabile and Steven Kramer at Harvard Business School, found that people who set challenging but achievable goals were more likely to be creative and productive than those who set easy or difficult goals.[7]

So, let's review: *Specific* goals are clear and unambiguous. They communicate to both you and your coach exactly what needs to be accomplished. *Measurable* goals can be quantified. This makes it possible to track progress and determine whether or not the goal has been met. *Achievable* goals are realistic times on your calendar that can be accomplished within specific time frames. They are not so easy that they are boring, but not so difficult that they are impossible. *Relevant* goals are aligned with your overall goals and objectives while providing the motivation and passion to act as your catalyst. They are not simply busy work but are steps toward achieving something that evokes passion and meaning. *Timely* goals have a deadline. This helps you stay focused and motivated.

---

6 Gardner, Sarah and Albee, Dave, "Goal-setting research cited by TIME, Forbes, Yahoo, others" (2016). News. 3. https://scholar.dominican.edu/news-releases/3

7 Amabile, Teresa M., and Steve J. Kramer. *The Progress Principle: Using Small Wins to Ignite Joy, Engagement, and Creativity at Work.* Harvard Business Review Press, 2011.

SMART goals make it easier for you to track progress, stay motivated, and adjust as needed. Most importantly, they allow both you and your coach to develop accountability standards that work best for your ongoing relationship. This is essential to ensure follow-through and it promotes a clear understanding of what needs to be done and when it needs to be done by. This kind of relationship also helps you become more willing to accept feedback and constructive criticism, enhancing the likelihood that your goals will be achieved.

I have provided you with a template to help you complete a SMART plan. Try to be objective about your inherent weaknesses that may be caused by your strengths. Once the top section of the SMART plan is completed from the results of your assessments, you will have a guideline for what may inhibit the success or lack of attainment of your goals.

Once again, here are the guidelines for making your plan SMART:

- **Specific** – If your goal is to develop assertiveness skills, specify exactly the skills on which you need to focus. If you are **not** specific, your chance of achieving your goals is minimal.
- **Measurable** – You must know what the specific steps you are about to take will look like once you complete it. If you are going to read a book, identify the number of chapters and divide that into the number of days or weeks until you have to complete it. Then identify what the daily steps look like, how it can be measured while calculating "life gets in the way" time.

- **Achievable –** To figure out when and how you can achieve your goals, it's crucial to have both the time and the resources. Make sure you believe that with reasonable effort, reaching your milestone is possible in that time frame. Check your schedule and set aside a specific time to concentrate on your objective. Make an appointment with yourself (and others if needed) and commit to keeping that appointment no matter what!
- **Relevant –** Your goals must be YOUR goals. They must be based on YOUR desires, not those of your parents, your relatives, or your spouse. Your behaviors, capacities, and values will direct you toward something unique and specific to you.
- **Timely –** If you do not set time parameters, your plan will never occur. There will ALWAYS be something urgent about to happen requiring your attention. You must be objective—know when the process starts and when it ends. Give the dates and time involvement. When the time comes, finish up and move on.

Now, here's an example:

Summarise your strengths:

A People orientation with strong interpersonal skills

B Loyal to company but committed to family as well

C Optimistic with ability to encourage and focus on the task at hand

D Strong beliefs, called to lead and love others

Summarise your weaknesses:

A Not very objective about goals

B Lack strong practicality

C May not remain on tasks for very long, keeping me from competence at times.

D I am oblivious to much of what is going on or the way things may appear

	Specific	Measurable	Attainable	Relevant	Timely
Personal Applications	I will make sure that I improve my health because it is beginning to have an impact on my quality of life	I will lose 20 pounds and improve my cardio-vascular health through aerobics	I will reduce my calorie intake and exercise three times a week with a friend who has similar goals	Attending sessions will give an opportunity to create new relationship and improve my self-esteem and appearance	I will achieve this weight loss and health improvement by December 31st of this year.
Professional Applications	I will renew my Senior Professional Human Resources designation through independent study	I will need to take a minimum of 30 hours of course instruction in strategic planning, benefits and labour law.	I will sign up for the Human Resource Institute's structured program to guide me through the process	To keep my status as a human resource manager I want to remain qualified and address my weaknesses in strategic planning.	I have six months to complete the course so I must finish 1 class per month. I will target the 15th of each month to complete

It is my hope that once you have completed this process you will continue to use a SMART Personal Development Plan as a means of helping you achieve short, medium, and long-term goals. You can use your present analysis as a foundation at that time.

I don't want you to think I'm being redundant, but **Celebrating Achievements** is an important part of accountability and follow-through. It helps acknowledge progress, boosts motivation, and strengthens the collaborative relationship between you and your coach. Recognizing and celebrating progress allows both of you to stay motivated and focused on your respective roles and goals. It also helps you build self-efficacy and confidence, which are essential to your long-term success. Celebrating Achievements, as we have stressed in the past, is an important part of accountability and follow-through.

Additionally, your self-esteem will often increase when you achieve a goal, because you have proven to yourself that you are capable of achieving things. This helps motivate you to achieve future goals. Achieving a goal will also give you a sense of momentum and motivation, which can make you more likely to set and achieve more goals in the future.

Key Insights

Accountability and follow-through are essential to being coachable and achieving personal and professional growth. By setting clear goals, developing a plan, establishing deadlines, holding yourself accountable, and celebrating achievements, you can develop the mindset and habits needed for success. With practice and effort, you will learn to be accountable and follow through on your commitments.

Case Study: Ben

When Ben first came to me, he was frustrated after multiple failed attempts to lose weight and get back in shape. At the time, the annual "River Run 5K" was about four months away and his friends were berating him because he had not participated with them for the past few years. He felt that only through some sort of coaching and accountability would he manage to get back into a healthy routine, because joining the gym simply wasn't working.

After a couple of sessions, I asked him this: "Your goal is to lose 15 pounds, run a 5k, and have regular visualization sessions to get your rhythm back. How are you doing on those goals?" His reply was "I'm doing pretty well on the weight loss goal. I've been tracking my calories and exercising regularly. I'm down 5 pounds so far."

"That's great! Keep up the good work. How about the running goal?"

Ben said: "I've been running 3 times a week, but I haven't been able to run a 5k yet. I'm getting closer though. I ran 3 miles last week. I just get tired and really can't seem to find the motivation to push through. I'm just not sure I can do this."

My reply was: "That's progress! Keep at it and you'll be running a 5k in no time. How about your visualizations? Are you getting away to a quiet, undisturbed place and seeing yourself hit that finish line ahead of your friends?"

"I've been making good progress on that too, but not daily."

"That sounds great! You are better off than you were several weeks ago. It's important to continue to celebrate your achievements along the way, even if they are not on a daily basis. When you reach a goal, take some time to reflect on your progress and how you feel." I also challenged Ben to call his buddies and ask them if he could run with them, since that could help Ben stay motivated and keep moving forward. "It's obvious these friends are important to you, or you would not be motivated to join them in the River Run. Call them today and find out where they are meeting for their sessions and join them."

For Ben, this seemed to turn on the light bulb. He called his friend and started meeting with the group. His wife encouraged him each night after dinner to "go visualize crossing the finish line," which he did. On race day, he achieved his goal—and he actually beat a couple of the guys in the group!

Reflection Questions:

1. What are some common barriers to accountability?

2. How can you hold yourself accountable?

3. In what ways can an accountability partner or coach help you stay accountable?

4. What are some strategies for following through on commitments?

5. How can you balance accountability with self-compassion?

How can you take steps to develop accountability and follow-through during the coaching process?

1. **Reflect on growth:** Take the time to reflect on your journey and growth. Recognize your growth and progress—not just the outcome but also the efforts and development that led to the achievement.

2. Make sure your coach, family member, friend, or counselor is **actively listening** to you and applauds your goal achievements. Let your coach know how you would like to celebrate these achievements. It could be a verbal acknowledgment, a written note, or something else.

3. **Set new goals:** Celebrations should also serve as a stepping stone for setting new goals and challenges. Use the achievement as a springboard to reach even greater heights, explore new possibilities, and set new targets.

4. **Maintain balance:** Celebrations should be enjoyable and meaningful but should not become the focus. Don't let your celebrations overshadow the ongoing coaching process and the focus on continuous improvement—the ultimate goal.

CHAPTER 11

LEARNING FROM FAILURE

Failure is an inevitable part of life, but it can also be a valuable learning experience. The greatest advantage of learning from failure is that it requires you to grow and develop as a person. When you fail, you are forced to confront your weaknesses and limitations. While this can be a painful experience, it is also a valuable learning opportunity. Reflecting on your failures can help you identify what went wrong and what you can do to improve. Through this process of self-reflection, you can become more resilient, adaptable and self-aware. In addition, learning from failure can help you to develop a growth mindset that equips you to persevere in the face of challenges and setbacks.

Most people learn more from failure than they do from doing things "right." Studies published by Carol Dweck at Stanford University, and Gail Matthews at Dominican University of California, found that people who reflect on their failures are more likely to achieve their goals and develop a growth mindset. People who took the time to reflect on their failures were more likely to identify the lessons they learned from their failures and use those lessons to improve their performance.

These studies suggest that both individual and team failure can be a valuable learning experience. When you fail, you have the opportunity to identify your weaknesses, learn from your mistakes, and develop new strategies for success. If you can learn to embrace failure and see it as an opportunity to learn and grow, you can become more successful in the long run.

When leaders empower their team members, especially after mistakes, it demonstrates a belief in everyone's abilities and gives them a sense of ownership and control over their work and decisions. When people feel empowered, they are more likely to be motivated, engaged, and committed to their tasks.

Building autonomy and trust fosters a more positive culture where you are more likely to take risks, learn from your mistakes, and contribute your unique perspectives. When you feel valued and confident in your abilities, it leads to stronger relationships, collaboration, and overall organizational success.

The first step in learning from failure is reframing it, which means you change your perspective. This allows you to see these events as opportunities for growth and learning. Without reframing failure, you may be more likely to give up when encountering setbacks. You may also be more likely to dwell on mistakes and let them discourage you. Reframing failure helps you see those mistakes in a positive light rather than a negative one.

Failure is not a reflection of one's worth or abilities but rather a chance to learn and improve. Some of the most brilliant people leading organizations only have a productive decision rate of 71%, according to the late Dr. R. Chris Martin of the University of Missouri - Kansas City. It is normal to feel disappointed, frustrated, or even angry when you fail. Allow yourself to feel these emotions, but don't let them consume you. Take the time to identify what went wrong after processing your emotions. Ask yourself: "What could I have done differently?" or "What did I learn from the experience?"

After asking yourself these questions, don't beat yourself up over your mistakes. Instead, use them as an opportunity to learn and grow through hard work and effort. Focus on the positive aspects of your experience. What did you achieve? How did you grow as a person? By answering these questions, you can become more resilient, adaptable, and successful.

Once failure occurs, it's important to analyze it and identify areas for improvement. Analysis helps uncover the fundamental reasons behind the failure, including any systemic issues, process flaws, or human errors. This is valuable knowledge. Both you and/or your coach will gain insights that you can apply in order to improve performance and minimize the risk of repeating the same mistakes in your future endeavors.

Analyzing failure also fosters a problem-solving mindset. It encourages critical thinking and finding alternative solutions or approaches to address challenges or mitigate risks. Through this process, individuals and organizations can develop more robust strategies and responses to potential failures.

Additionally, analyzing your failures provides valuable information that strengthens your decision-making skills. As a result, you can make better-informed choices, implement appropriate risk management measures, and adjust your strategies, plans, or processes to increase the likelihood of success.

Another critically important benefit of analysis is that it encourages innovation and continuous improvement by fostering a mentality of exploration. Experimenting with new ideas, being willing to take calculated risks, and identifying areas for improvement can help you develop better products, services, or processes. Above all, innovation helps build your resilience and adaptability while developing a mindset that embraces challenges. By learning from your setbacks and adapting your strategies to changing circumstances, you'll increase your ability to bounce back and thrive in the face of adversity.

Previously, we talked about the necessity of feedback. Feedback is an essential tool for learning from failure. It helps you gain a new perspective and identify blind spots that may have contributed to past failure. Approach feedback with an open mind and a willingness to learn—otherwise, you are destined to keep repeating the same mistakes. This cycle of failure can be difficult to break, leading to a loss of confidence and motivation. You may even start to believe that you are not capable of achieving your goals.

Learning from failure requires taking action. It means you must actively engage in the process of reflection, adaptation, and improvement; otherwise, you may dwell on the pain or confusion and feel demoralized. By taking action, you can experiment with different approaches and strategies, gather feedback, and make necessary adjustments based on the lessons learned from your failures.

Taking action can give you valuable insights into what works and what doesn't. You can then identify areas for improvement or develop alternative solutions. This proactive approach helps you refine your skills, knowledge, and decision-making abilities. This can inspire you to develop a plan for improvement, set new goals, and take steps to implement change. By acting, you can turn failure into a catalyst for growth and development.

Practice Self-Compassion: Finally, it's important to practice self-compassion when learning from failure. This means being kind to yourself and recognizing that failure is a natural part of the learning process. When you do not practice self-compassion when learning from failure, you are more likely to experience negative emotions such as shame, guilt, or self-doubt. These emotions make it difficult to learn from your mistakes and move on. In addition, not practicing self-compassion can lead to a cycle of self-criticism and negative self-talk, which damages your self-esteem and makes it difficult to cope with setbacks.

Refusing to practice self-compassion erects formidable barriers to personal growth. Without self-compassion, individuals often cultivate a fixed mindset, staunchly believing in their inherent limitations rather than embracing the potential for change. This mindset rigidifies neural pathways, hindering the brain's natural ability to adapt and rewire itself—a process known as neuroplasticity. Moreover, the absence of self-compassion can influence epigenetic processes, as chronic stress and negative self-perception trigger biochemical reactions that impact gene expression. Over time, this can lead to detrimental health outcomes and further reinforce a stagnant worldview. Embracing self-compassion, however, nurtures a growth mindset, fostering resilience and enabling the brain and body to thrive through flexible adaptation and positive genetic expression.

When you are not compassionate with yourself, you are less likely to believe in your ability to succeed. This can lead to reduced motivation and a sense of hopelessness. That is no way to live! You were designed with unique abilities and strengths; by embracing and applying them, you can make a positive impact in your family, your workplace, the wider community, and even the world.

Key Insights

Learning from failure is an essential part of your personal and professional growth. By reframing failure as an opportunity for growth, analyzing the failure, embracing feedback, taking action, and practicing self-compassion, you can turn failure into a stepping stone toward success. With a growth mindset and a willingness to learn, you'll be ready to see failure as a tool for growth and development.

Never forget this quote by Alexander Pope from the early 18th century: "To err is human; to forgive, divine." Forgiveness is not just something we do for others; it is something we must also do for ourselves! It allows us to pursue a positive relationship with ourselves which, in turn, creates a mindset of freedom.

Case Study: Lessons from a Bestselling Author

Once upon a time, J. K. Rowling, author of the Harry Potter series, was rejected by multiple publishing houses. Some of them even suggested that she should give up writing. However, instead of letting failure deter her, she chose to reframe it as an opportunity to improve her work. She analyzed the feedback she received and used it to refine her manuscript and storytelling techniques.

Moreover, Rowling's ability to receive feedback played a crucial role in her growth as a writer. She was open to constructive criticism and took it as a chance to learn and develop her skills. She sought input from editors and trusted individuals who helped her shape the story and make it more compelling.

Throughout her journey, Rowling faced personal challenges, including financial difficulties and the loss of her mother. However, she practiced self-compassion by acknowledging her own worth and not letting setbacks define her. She continued to persevere and believe in her abilities, using her passion for writing as a source of strength and motivation.

Ultimately, J. K. Rowling's resilience—as well as her ability to reframe failure, analyze feedback, and practice self-compassion—allowed her to overcome obstacles and achieve tremendous success as a world-renowned author. Her story serves as an inspiring example of how one can learn and grow from failure through a combination of determination and self-reflection.

Reflection Questions:

1. What are some common misconceptions about failure?

2. How can you learn from failure without dwelling on it?

3. How can a coach or mentor help you learn from failure?

4. What is the difference between constructive criticism and negative feedback?

5. What are some examples of successful people who have learned from failure?

Have you taken the steps necessary to learn from failure during the coaching process?

1. Are you allowing yourself to feel disappointment, but not allowing those feelings to consume you?

2. Do you feel comfortable asking yourself what you could have done differently? Or what did you learn from the experience?

3. After less than favorable results, do you still have the belief in yourself that can help you to persevere in the face of challenges and setbacks?

4. Are you focusing on the positive? Rather than dwelling on your failures, can you identify any positive aspects of your experience? What did you learn? What did you achieve? How did you grow as a person?

5. Do you solicit feedback from people you trust about your failure?

CHAPTER 12

BUILDING A SUPPORT NETWORK

Having a strong support network is essential for being coachable as it provides emotional encouragement, empathy, and understanding, helping you navigate life's ups and downs and the stresses that come with the coaching process. Without such a network, you might feel isolated or overwhelmed, affecting your ability to achieve your objectives. A robust support system keeps you accountable for your goals and commitments, offering diverse perspectives and constructive feedback. It also builds confidence and provides motivation, especially when tackling unfamiliar tasks or finding effective solutions.

A strong support network facilitates connections, widening access to resources and opportunities for collaboration. It helps you leverage new opportunities, partnerships, or mentorship possibilities, and provides a buffer to help you bounce back from setbacks. This chapter explores building a network of supportive individuals who offer necessary guidance and encouragement. The first step is identifying your needs, such as guidance, motivation, or accountability, which enables you to target individuals who can provide specific support.

Reflect on the type of people who can best meet your needs by asking what kind of support you require, whether it's someone to talk to or help with practical tasks. Plan where to find these individuals and make it a project to build a network that can help you achieve your goals. Building a support network takes time and effort, but it is crucial for your coaching journey and overall success.

Once you've identified your needs, begin building a support network by meeting new people through clubs, classes, or volunteering. Be genuine and authentic, as people connect better with those who are real. Be patient, as building a support network takes time and involves multiple steps. Keep engaging with new people, and eventually, you'll find those who are right for you.

Reaching out to others, such as mentors, colleagues, or friends, positions you with access to needed resources and support. Having people who cheer you on and hold you accountable increases your chances of success and helps you stay motivated during tough times. Respecting others builds trust and shows your willingness to learn and grow, encouraging mutual respect in your relationships.

Scan here!

Building a support network requires investing time in relationships and understanding how to communicate effectively with different types of people. Tools like the LifeThrive Behavior and Values Assessment (https://www.lifethrive.com/behavior-and-values-assessment/)

can provide insights into communication preferences. Recognizing your own style helps you appreciate differences in others. Overcoming fears of rejection and social discomfort is crucial, as many experienced individuals are eager to connect. Remember, persistence leads to finding meaningful relationships that enhance your life and help you achieve your goals.

Building a support network is not just about receiving support but also about offering it. By supporting others, you can build strong relationships and develop a sense of reciprocity. This means being willing to listen, offer advice, and provide encouragement when needed. Here are ten suggestions that can help you be supportive to others:

1. Listen actively; offer a safe and non-judgmental space for others to express themselves.

2. Offer words of encouragement by letting people know that you believe in them and their abilities.

3. Demonstrate consistency in your actions and follow through on your commitments.

4. Identify specific ways in which you can assist others based on your expertise.

5. Show empathy and understanding. Avoid dismissing or belittling the other person's feelings.

6. Accept people for who they are, without passing judgment.

7. Be present. Make yourself available to listen and provide support when needed.

8. Provide information and guidance to aid in someone else's personal and professional development.

9. Share in their joy and let them know that their achievements matter to you.

10. Be open to fostering a mutually beneficial relationship where both parties can lean on each other as needed.

Finally, building a support network requires **maintaining connections**. This means staying in touch with others and nurturing the relationship over time. You should reach out regularly as well, not waiting on them to call. Also, try to find time for face-to-face interactions. Schedule regular get-togethers like coffee dates, lunches, or walks in the park.

When your support network members are going through tough times, be there for them. Offer them your support and encouragement and don't be afraid to share your thoughts and feelings. An effective support network is built on the principle of reciprocity or mutual assistance. Finally, don't forget to show up with an attitude of gratitude; thank them for being there for you.

When you build quality relationships with others, good things are bound to happen! Your network will be ever-expanding as you foster long-term relationships with people who are resourceful, supportive, and understanding. Even though life is full of changes and challenges, the wisdom and knowledge of others can enable you to adapt and remain resilient. With this foundation of confidence, you will be well prepared for whatever new opportunities life presents.

Identifying the RIGHT network

Accountability partners can be a valuable tool for enhancing coachability. This concept is summarized by the term "accountimacy," which, when fully grasped and applied, can accelerate your development more effectively than solely relying on a coach. Accountability is defined as an obligation to justify one's actions, ensuring they are evaluated and weighed for their value. Intimacy, on the other hand, refers to being closely acquainted with someone's innermost character, requiring vulnerability and careful selection of friends. Combining these terms, "accountimacy" is defined as an obligation to exchange satisfactory explanations for one's actions with someone who understands and empathizes with your innermost character.

Accountimacy involves bringing your coach, accountability partners, and trusted friends into a relationship where they are deeply invested in your well-being and goals. These individuals are passionate about the things you care about, remain by your side regardless of your decisions, and offer more support than superficial relationships. By being accessible, open, and vulnerable, you can cultivate the joy of accountimacy and develop deeper, more meaningful relationships. This state of security provides confidence and poise, enhancing your ability to navigate challenges.

To make the most of these key relationships, start by defining your goals and expectations clearly and communicating them to your inner circle. Ensure that your coach and accountimacy partners understand what you aim to achieve and how they can support you. This alignment will help you and your partners work together effectively, maximizing the benefits of accountimacy for your personal and professional growth.

Finding the right accountimacy partner

Bringing your coach, accountability partners, and trusted friends into a relationship based on accountimacy means having a support system deeply invested in your well-being and goals. These individuals are passionate about the things you care about and remain by your side regardless of your choices. They provide a level of care that surpasses that of acquaintances and professional relationships, offering unwavering support and encouragement.

To fully experience the benefits of accountimacy, you need to be accessible, approachable, open, and vulnerable. This fosters deeper, more meaningful relationships and leads to a sense of security, confidence, and poise under pressure. The key is to define your goals and expectations clearly and communicate them to all of those in your inner circle. This ensures everyone is aligned and can work together effectively to support your growth and development.

Choosing the right accountimacy partner involves finding someone with similar goals and values who is trustworthy, supportive, challenging, reliable, and encouraging. Regular check-ins are crucial for maintaining accountability and consistent interaction. These meetings provide the opportunity to discuss progress, challenges, and goals, keeping you on track and motivated. Having someone to answer to helps you stay focused and enhances your communication skills, increasing your chances of achieving your goals.

Key Insights

Building a support network is essential to being coachable and achieving personal and professional growth. By identifying your needs, reaching out to others, building relationships, offering support, and maintaining connections, you can build a strong support network that offers guidance and encouragement when you need it most. With the right Accountimacy partners in place, you can achieve your full potential.

Case Study: Sofia

Sofia was a brilliant young lady with above-average intelligence, but she was also struggling with anxiety and depression. She had big dreams and aspirations, but she often felt overwhelmed and unsure of how to achieve them. On top of that, Sofia had recently moved to our city for a job but didn't know anyone. She felt isolated and alone.

When I suggested that she start building a support network, Sofia seemed overwhelmed and very unsure of how to do that. I knew she could be quickly empowered if she developed a stronger personal and professional life. After a few thoughtful discussions, we discovered that she desired emotional support, motivation, and practical advice. Sofia started by reaching out to a team member, Lisa, with whom she shared many interests in common. Lisa not only provided a listening ear but also offered words of encouragement and reminded Sofia of her strengths. This initial interaction deepened their friendship and laid the foundation for a stronger support network.

Recognizing the need for motivation, I encouraged Sofia to join a local networking group. In this group, she met John, and approached him by sharing her aspirations. Impressed by Sofia's determination, John offered to become her mentor. Through John's mentorship, Sofia gained the motivation and guidance she needed to navigate her professional journey.

As Sofia's support network grew, she realized the importance of reciprocity and giving back to others. She started volunteering at a local community center, where she met Anna, a single mother striving to balance work and family. Sofia empathized with Anna's struggles and offered her support. They soon developed a deep bond and began regularly exchanging advice, resources, and emotional support. Sofia's willingness to help Anna not only strengthened their friendship but also enriched Sofia's own life.

As Sofia's journey progressed and she became an integral part of an expanding support network, she found herself transformed. The once overwhelmed and uncertain woman had grown into a confident and empowered individual, surrounded by a network of like-minded individuals. Together, they celebrated victories, weathered challenges, and lifted each other up.

Reflection Question:

1. Why is it important to have a support network?

2. How can you maintain relationships with members of your support network?

3. What role does vulnerability play in building a support network?

4. What are some common misconceptions about building a support network?

5. How can you show gratitude to members of your support network?

6. What are some qualities to look for in an accountimacy partner?

7. What role does trust play in an accountimacy partnership?

What steps have you taken to build a support network during the coaching process?

1. Have you considered areas where you require assistance or support?

2. What resources and support systems are already available to you?

3. Where do your existing support networks fall short?

4. What qualities would you like to see in your potential new supporters?

5. Who belongs in your mutually beneficial support network?

6. Do you feel concerned about open and honest communication with your accountimacy partner?

7. Would this team of accountimacy partners help you celebrate achievements, offer assistance when needed, and provide constructive feedback?

CHAPTER 13

PUTTING IT ALL TOGETHER

Perhaps you're familiar with this phrase: *"Tell them what you're going to tell them, tell them and tell them what you've told them."* As you consider what you have learned in this book about the characteristics of coachability, hopefully you will realize that these characteristics can apply to multiple areas of your life and that many of the concepts are intertwined and dependent on one another.

The six dimensions of coachability that were measured on your Coachability Index—Expressed Humility, Motivation, Seeking Feedback, Receptivity to Feedback, Response Motive, and Response to Feedback—have all been addressed in various ways throughout this book. Please take the time to dig into each of these dimensions and how they can impact the discovery, growth and development processes you will encounter during your coaching journey.

In this final chapter, you'll see all the concepts discussed throughout the book tied together. Although this chapter may appear to be repetitive, there is purpose behind it. Solidifying these principles in your mind will help you maximize your potential and achieve the objectives you dream of. Your desires are there for a reason—they were implanted in your psyche to push you toward your purpose in life. A strong sense of purpose helps you achieve the direction and peace you have the capacity for and inspires you to continue growing and developing your skills over time.

Highlight Reel: The Keys to Being Coachable

The first step in becoming more coachable is to assess your current state. This means reflecting on your strengths and weaknesses and identifying areas for improvement. This is most easily accomplished by completing a few assessments that are easily accessi-

Scan here!

ble. To get an in-depth understanding of your capabilities, you may want to invest in a more thorough tool (at https://www.lifethrive.com/tti-talent-insights/) to learn more about your behavioral tendencies as well as your strongest priorities and motivations in life. If you are on a shoestring budget, consider taking the *free* Behavior and Values Assessment available on the LifeThrive website (https://www.lifethrive.com/behavior-and-values-assessment/). While not comprehensive, it can help you and your coach identify general tendencies in your personality that will impact your life and relationships.

Scan here!

If you are reading this book, there is a good chance you have already taken the LifeThrive Coachability Index (https://www. lifethrive.com/coachability-assessment/). But if you have not, and you are serious about the process of becoming more coachable, it is a

Scan here!

robust assessment that will show you exactly where you may excel or struggle during the coaching process. The results will help you AND your coach gain a more focused direction to maximize your time together.

Second, if you are willing to invest in a coach, they will expect you to develop a growth mindset. It is essential to being coachable. When you possess humility and have a growth mindset, you are more likely to be receptive to a coach's feedback. In addition, you'll likely be more motivated to make efforts to improve. This can lead to faster and more significant progress, especially if you are willing to learn from your mistakes.

As a reminder, a growth mindset is the belief that intelligence and abilities are not fixed—rather, they can be developed through hard work and effort. That type of humility allows you to see challenges as opportunities for learning and growth rather than as threats. When you have a growth mindset, you are also more likely to persist in the face of setbacks, and to learn from your mistakes. By developing a growth mindset, you can overcome obstacles and achieve your full potential.

Third, both seeking feedback and responding to feedback are key aspects of being coachable. This means being open to constructive criticism and using it as an opportunity for growth and development. When you approach feedback with an open mind and a willingness to learn, it will improve your motivation and allow you to make significant progress more quickly. Being open to feedback also increases your self-confidence and resilience while allowing you to build improved relationships with others. As that occurs, you'll also benefit from steadily growing emotional intelligence.

When you have a strong response motive and are willing to put feedback into action, you can build a very strong support network. Building this network is essential to being coachable—and it can be your lifeline to wise guidance and encouragement. Your support network should include "accountimacy" partners who are not merely acquaintances, but people who have a desire to see you succeed. It's important to invest in these relationships and offer support in return. Never discount the valuable information that others can share with you, even if they are not your favorite person.

You have also learned why you should apply SMART goals to your coaching process. If you truly want to pursue growth through coaching, work with a coach who can help you set goals that are Specific, Measurable, Attainable, Relevant and Timely. Learning to identify SMART goals can help keep your coaching process on track and ensure that you are progressing toward your goals. More importantly, SMART goals are easier to manage because they break down the objectives into manageable steps that help keep you focused and not overwhelmed.

Holding yourself accountable is another essential component to being coachable. By hiring a coach, you are investing in yourself and that should provide the motivation to be a good steward to your investment. By accepting your coach's direction, taking responsibility for your actions and decisions, and being willing to accept feedback and criticism, you will quickly develop your pathway to success.

If you are *not* pursuing accountability during the coaching process, here are some of the challenges you could encounter:

1. You may struggle to make meaningful progress toward your goals. You might find it difficult to take consistent action, follow through on commitments, and implement the necessary changes discussed in the coaching sessions.

2. You may overlook or dismiss amazing opportunities, limiting your potential for growth and improvement.

3. Accountability helps challenge and modify negative patterns of behavior or thinking. Lacking accountability causes you to maintain self-limiting beliefs that hinder your development.

4. Accountability creates a sense of responsibility and motivation to achieve your desired outcomes. Without accountability, your motivation may wane, leading to a lack of drive and enthusiasm for making positive changes.

5. Accountability is a fundamental aspect of the coaching relationship. Not having this strain, the relationship with your coach can hinder the trust and rapport necessary for productive sessions.

As we mentioned in Chapter 4, humility is the strongest and most determining factor when it comes to being coachable. Humility helps you open your own limited view to new ideas and learn from your mistakes—which are often the best learning experiences. Learning from mistakes is an essential part of being coachable. This means reframing failure as an opportunity for growth and development, analyzing the failure, and taking action to improve. And the only way to ensure you deepen your level of expressed humility is by developing accountimacy partners who will be honest with you because they genuinely care about you as an individual and your success. If they won't tell you the truth, are they really your friend?

Celebrating achievements is another key to being coachable. By expressing your humility and willingness to learn, you open your own limited view to new ideas and learn from your mistakes through your neuroplasticity. Then epigenetics can kick in and provide you with a new capacity to express yourself and your actions which often provides the best learning experiences.

Key Insights

Becoming more coachable requires effort, practice, and a willingness to learn and grow. If you have not already, identify areas that need to be addressed based on your Coachability Index. Consider which aspects of your makeup need work:

1. Identify your intrapersonal strengths and weaknesses by clarifying your level of expressed humility. If it's low, you will want to deepen your accountimacy network and do your best to follow your coach's direction. If your motivation level is

low, you probably have a propensity to hesitate to act which will require that your coach and accountimacy network ensure that you maintain timely responses and a sense of urgency.

2. Recognize the value of exchanging your thoughts, ideas, and objectives with others by seeking feedback and responding to it as quickly as possible. No one has all the answers, so it behooves you to seek out other's experiences and wisdom. But you cannot just be a seeker, you must also be receptive to that feedback, especially if the person providing it has knowledge and experience that you do not possess.

3. Determine the strength of your motivation to accept and apply what others share with you. If your response motive is low, you must look inside and determine how much passion you have for the objective you have on the table. Then you must take that passion and become an implementer by responding to that feedback. Otherwise, it is like an idea that is never put into action and most often that is from a lack of passion for the final result.

Now that you have taken a deep dive into your motivation and seeking the direction you need you will be ready to begin the first step toward your objectives and success. By assessing your current state, developing a growth mindset, seeking feedback, building a support network, setting goals and establishing deadlines, holding yourself accountable, learning from failure, and celebrating achievements, you can become more coachable and achieve your full potential. With the right mindset and habits in place, you will learn to be coachable and achieve your goals.

Now is your time. Your objectives are waiting to be grasped. The *you* that you always wanted to be is waiting, so what are you waiting for?

Reflection Questions:

1. What concepts from this book resonated with you the most?

2. In what ways can you hold yourself accountable for implementing what you've learned?

3. How can you measure your progress in becoming a more coachable person?

4. What are some of the barriers to implementing what you've learned? How can you overcome them?

5. How can you stay motivated and committed to being a more coachable person?

Have you taken the steps necessary to build your capacity to be coachable? Since you began this book, have you determined:

1. How can you increase your humility?

2. How to conquer fear?

3. How to choose a coach?

4. How to develop a growth mindset and learn from failure?

5. How can self-talk help you build resilience?

6. What approaches can you use to deal with change?

7. How to build a support network?

8. How to balance self-reflection and feedback?

SUGGESTED READING

Chapter 1: The Importance of Being Coachable
- *The Coaching Habit: Say Less, Ask More & Change the Way You Lead Forever* by Michael Bungay Stanier
- *Mindset: The New Psychology of Success* by Carol S. Dweck
- *The Power of Positive Leadership: How and Why Positive Leaders Transform Teams and Organizations and Change the World* by Jon Gordon
- *The Compound Effect* by Darren Hardy
- *The 7 Habits of Highly Effective People* by Stephen Covey

Chapter 2: The Characteristics of a Coachable Person
- *The Four Agreements: A Practical Guide to Personal Freedom* by Don Miguel Ruiz
- *Daring Greatly: How the Courage to Be Vulnerable Transforms the Way We Live, Love, Parent, and Lead* by Brené Brown
- *The Alchemist* by Paulo Coelho

- *The Lean Startup: How Today's Entrepreneurs Use Continuous Innovation to Create Radically Successful Businesses* by Eric Ries
- *The Art of Possibility: Transforming Professional and Personal Life* by Rosamund Stone Zander and Benjamin Zander

Chapter 3: Cultivating Self-awareness: the first step to emotional intelligence and growth

- *Coaching for Performance* by John Whitmore
- *The Handbook of Knowledge-Based Coaching: From Theory to Practice* by Leni Wildflower and Diane Brennan
- *Assessing Emotional Intelligence: Theory, Research, and Applications* by Con Stough, Donald H. Saklofske, and James D.A. Parker
- *Psychological Testing: Principles, Applications, and Issues* by Robert M. Kaplan and Dennis P. Saccuzzo
- *Assessment and Coaching: Theoretical Foundations and Practical Applications* by Philippe Rosinski and David B. Drake
- *The Coaching Process: A Practical Guide to Becoming an Effective Sports Coach* by Lynn Kidman and Stephanie J. Hanrahan
- *Coaching Psychology Manual* by Margaret Moore, Bob Tschannen-Moran, and Gloria Silverio

Chapter 4: The Role of Humility in Personal and Professional Growth

- *Humilitas: A Lost Key to Life, Love, and Leadership* by John Dickson
- *The Obstacle Is the Way: The Timeless Art of Turning Trials into Triumph* by Ryan Holiday
- *Good to Great: Why Some Companies Make the Leap and Others Don't* by Jim Collins
- *The Art of Possibility: Transforming Professional and Personal Life* by Rosamund Stone Zander and Benjamin Zander
- *The Road Less Traveled: A New Psychology of Love, Traditional Values and Spiritual Growth* by M. Scott Peck

Chapter 5: Overcoming the Fear of Feedback

- *Thanks for the Feedback: The Science and Art of Receiving Feedback Well* by Douglas Stone and Sheila Heen
- *Crucial Conversations: Tools for Talking When Stakes Are High* by Kerry Patterson, Joseph Grenny, Ron McMillan, and Al Switzler
- *Radical Candor: Be a Kick-Ass Boss Without Losing Your Humanity* by Kim Scott
- *The 5 AM Club: Own Your Morning, Elevate Your Life* by Robin Sharma
- *The Subtle Art of Not Giving a F*ck: A Counterintuitive Approach to Living a Good Life* by Mark Manson

Chapter 6: Seeking Out the Right Coach or Mentor

- *The Mentor Leader: Secrets to Building People and Teams That Win Consistently* by Tony Dungy
- *The Third Door: The Wild Quest to Uncover How the World's Most Successful People Launched Their Careers* by Alex Banayan
- *The Lean Startup: How Today's Entrepreneurs Use Continuous Innovation to Create Radically Successful Businesses* by Eric Ries
- *The Art of Possibility: Transforming Professional and Personal Life* by Rosamund Stone Zander and Benjamin Zander
- *The Talent Code: Greatness Isn't Born. It's Grown. Here's How.* by Daniel Coyle

Chapter 7: Embracing a Growth Mindset

- *Mindset: The New Psychology of Success* by Carol S. Dweck
- *Atomic Habits: An Easy & Proven Way to Build Good Habits & Break Bad Ones* by James Clear
- *The Obstacle Is the Way: The Timeless Art of Turning Trials into Triumph* by Ryan Holiday
- *The Power of Positive Thinking* by Norman Vincent Peale
- *The Compound Effect* by Darren Hardy

Chapter 8: The Power of Positivity and Resilience

- *What to Say When You Talk to Yourself* by Shad Helmstetter
- *The Self-Talk Solution* by Shad Helmstetter
- *The Positive Power of Negative Thinking* by Julie K. Norem
- *As a Man Thinketh* by James Allen
- *The Magic of Thinking Big* by David J. Schwartz
- *Option B: Facing Adversity, Building Resilience, and Finding Joy* by Sheryl Sandberg and Adam Grant
- *Resilience: Hard-Won Wisdom for Living a Better Life* by Eric Greitens
- *The Resilience Factor: 7 Keys to Finding Your Inner Strength and Overcoming Life's Hurdles* by Karen Reivich and Andrew Shatté
- *The Art of Resilience: Strategies for an Unbreakable Mind and Body* by Ross Edgley
- *Mind Gym: An Athlete's Guide to Inner Excellence* by Gary Mack and David Casstevens

Chapter 9: Overcoming Resistance to Change

- *Who Moved My Cheese?* by Spencer Johnson
- *Switch: How to Change Things When Change Is Hard* by Chip Heath and Dan Heath
- *Atomic Habits: An Easy & Proven Way to Build Good Habits & Break Bad Ones* by James Clear
- *The Innovator's Dilemma: When New Technologies Cause Great Firms to Fail* by Clayton M. Christensen
- *Thinking, Fast and Slow* by Daniel Kahneman

Chapter 10: Accountability and Follow-Through

- *The Accountability Manifesto: How Accountability Helps You Stick to Goals* by S. J. Scott and Barrie Davenport
- *The One Thing: The Surprisingly Simple Truth Behind Extraordinary Results* by Gary Keller and Jay Papasan
- *The 12 Week Year: Get More Done in 12 Weeks than Others Do in 12 Months* by Brian P. Moran and Michael Lennington
- *Finish: Give Yourself the Gift of Done* by Jon Acuff
- *Eat That Frog! 21 Great Ways to Stop Procrastinating and Get More Done in Less Time* by Brian Tracy

Chapter 11: Learning from Failure

- *Failing Forward: Turning Mistakes into Stepping Stones for Success* by John C. Maxwell
- *The Art of Possibility: Transforming Professional and Personal Life* by Rosamund Stone Zander and Benjamin Zander
- *Mistakes Were Made (But Not by Me): Why We Justify Foolish Beliefs, Bad Decisions, and Hurtful Acts* by Carol Tavris and Elliot Aronson
- *The Lean Startup: How Today's Entrepreneurs Use Continuous Innovation to Create Radically Successful Businesses* by Eric Ries
- *Originals: How Non-Conformists Move the World* by Adam Grant

Chapter 12: Building a Support Network

- *Never Eat Alone: And Other Secrets to Success, One Relationship at a Time* by Keith Ferrazzi and Tahl Raz
- *The Art of Possibility: Transforming Professional and Personal Life* by Rosamund Stone Zander and Benjamin Zander
- *Crucial Conversations: Tools for Talking When Stakes Are High* by Kerry Patterson, Joseph Grenny, Ron McMillan, and Al Switzler
- *The Power of Moments: Why Certain Experiences Have Extraordinary Impact* by Chip Heath and Dan Heath
- *The Compound Effect* by Darren Hardy

Chapter 13: Putting It All Together

- *Atomic Habits: An Easy & Proven Way to Build Good Habits & Break Bad Ones* by James Clear
- *The 7 Habits of Highly Effective People* by Stephen Covey
- *The Compound Effect* by Darren Hardy
- *The Lean Startup: How Today's Entrepreneurs Use Continuous Innovation to Create Radically Successful Businesses* by Eric Ries
- *The Power of Positive Leadership: How and Why Positive Leaders Transform Teams and Organizations and Change the World* by Jon Gordon